Praise for
Be the Mom

As you read *Be the Mom*, you are going to be so encouraged. You are also going to love getting to know my friend Tracey Eyster. In a warm and welcoming style she invites us into her journey as a mom, winsomely reminding us of the unspeakable value of motherhood. As you read this book, you will find fresh hope that you can "be the mom"!

—BARBARA RAINEY, Co-Founder of FamilyLife, Speaker and Author
    of *Barbara & Susan's Guide to the Empty Nest*, Mother of six,
    Grandmother of nineteen

Tracey's exuberant personality shines through the pages of *Be the Mom*, infusing weary moms with practical help and encouragement to be the best moms they can be. I was inspired, challenged, and blessed while reading it!

—CRYSTAL PAINE, Money Saving Mom®, http://MoneySavingMom.com

Tracey's contagious passion for motherhood gets under your skin when you read this book. It is a prescription for the apathetic attitude today's world breeds. She reminds you that we should be looking at motherhood as the greatest adventure and honor that it is.

—DANNAH GRESH, Author of *Six Ways to Keep the "Good" in Your Boy*

It's not often that I leap at the opportunity to write an endorsement for a book. I came out of my chair for *Be the Mom*. I am so excited about Tracey's writing and the encouragement she gives mothers that I'm buying a case and giving *Be the Mom*, first to my daughters and daughter-in-law, and then to a bunch of mothers who will benefit from learning from an authentic mom and mentor. *Be the Mom* is a great read!

—DR. DENNIS RAINEY, President of FamilyLife, Author of *Stepping Up:
    A Call to Courageous Manhood*

Tracey Eyster has written *the* book that most of us moms need to read. It's honest and straightforward, and it comes from a worldview that I understand and embrace. After 21 years in full-time radio, deciding to be a full-time mom to my young sons opened my eyes to the delights of motherhood and the challenges of balancing being a mom with a host of other things. For me, Tracey's book *Be the Mom* is a direct answer to prayer. She speaks to the hearts of moms, offering wise advice and lots of encouragement. She is a mentor-friend for all of us.

—LISA WILLIAMS, Former National K-LOVE Morning Show Host

Laugh and learn! Fresh, frank, and funny, *Be the Mom* is a great resource to encourage you on your momlife journey, and to help you steer clear of those nasty mom traps along the way.

—MARY A. KASSIAN, Author of *Girls Gone Wise in a World Gone Wild*

I know Tracey Eyster and have admired her passion and zeal for helping moms to be the best they can be. Motherhood has never been harder. Pitfalls are everywhere. What is needed is wise encouragement from an honest, authentic life. Tracey Eyster can offer you both. I highly recommend her book, *Be the Mom.*

—ROBERT LEWIS, Pastor and Creator of the Men's Fraternity Series,
Author of *Raising a Modern-Day Knight*

In the pages of this book, you'll find profound wisdom, packaged lightheartedly, that will encourage, inspire, and equip you at the deepest level. Even as I chuckled at her stories, I found myself reaching for my pen to take notes over and over again. I found tears leaking from my eyes at the sheer, awe-inspiring vision God gives women for motherhood. Tracey's book is an invaluable tool to help mothers "be the mom" that God has designed us to be.

—SHAUNTI FELDHAHN, Social Researcher, Speaker, and Best-Selling
Author of *For Women Only* and *For Parents Only*

be the
mom

TRACEY LANTER EYSTER

Tyndale House Publishers, Inc.
Carol Stream, Illinois

Editor: Brandy Bruce
Cover design by Jacqueline L. Nuñez
Cover photograph copyright © Agnieszka Kirinicjanow/iStockphoto. All rights reserved.

The author is represented by the literary agency of Wolgemuth & Associates.

Library of Congress Cataloging-in-Publication Data
Eyster, Tracey Lanter.
  Be the mom / Tracey Lanter Eyster.
     p. cm.
  Includes bibliographical references (p.   ) and index.
  ISBN 978-1-58997-684-9 (alk. paper)
  1. Mothers—Religious life. 2. Motherhood—Religious aspects—Christianity. 3. Motherhood—Psychology. I. Title.
  BV4529.18.E97 2012
  248.8'431—dc23

                          2012010893

Printed in the United States of America

4 5 6 7 8 9 / 18 17 16 15 14

To Samara and Westley, my God gifts!

○   ○   ○

Trust God from the bottom of your heart; don't try to
figure out everything on your own. Listen for
God's voice in everything you do, everywhere you go;
he's the one who will keep you on track.
—Proverbs 3:5-6, THE MESSAGE

Contents

Acknowledgments

God has put together an amazing and unexplainable set of circumstances (that only He could have) to birth, grow, and launch *Be the Mom*. Not the least of which is my being blessed to be a mom through the miracle of two pregnancies that were not supposed to occur.

My heart is filled with gratitude to Dennis and Barbara Rainey for seeing something in Bill and me that we didn't see in ourselves when they plucked us from the corporate world and charged us to join with them in building strong marriages and families. Our lives and our children's lives are fuller because of you. Thank you.

Tim Grissom, I appreciate your guidance and the care you took in coaching me through those beginning steps of the process. You boosted my confidence at just the right time. Thank you to Andrew Wolgemuth, my agent, for supporting and handholding this first-time author. You are awesome! Brandy Bruce, my editor, has been tenacious in her attention to detail and steadfast in her efforts to draw more out of me than I knew was in there! Thanks, Brandy, for going the extra mile and helping me craft the words from my heart to the page.

To my sweet cheerleader friends who fully understand the struggles of penning a book and spoke words of encouragement over me and spurred me on—thanks, Susan, Shaunti, Dannah, and Crystal! Linda Treadway, Suzanne Thomas, and Katie Howard Clemens—you three blessed me continuously as you stepped in to cover all the bases at MomLife Today while I put in the hours at the keyboard!

Extra special thanks to my prayer warriors, Craig and Dianne Bias, Doug and Deb Gulbranson, Rich and Mary Jensen, and Julie Denker, who answered e-mail requests, sent "You can do it!" texts, and asked consistently, "How's it going? How can we pray?" Your prayers carried me over the rough spots and kept me believing.

To my parents, Tod and Glenna, and my grandmothers, Sara and Velva, thank you for modeling love and commitment to your children.

Thanks to my daughter, Samara, who constantly encouraged my writing this book and offered just the right words when I struggled during the process. To my son, Westley, thanks for keeping me laughing on the days I was exhausted. You two have helped mold me as we lived this book out together, and I consider it all joy!

Every writer needs someone who really believes in them. For me, that has been my husband, Bill, and I am forever grateful to him. Bill, when I questioned the value of my voice, it was you who reminded me to fear God, not man. You're right, God asked me to write this book. It is now His, and together you and I will continue to pray that legacies will be strengthened through our life spilled onto these pages.

Preface

Be the Mom is a book for all moms, though it didn't start out that way. I began writing about my life experiences and the traps I found myself falling into so that one day I could pass them on to my young daughter when she enters motherhood. I wanted her to know that being a mom is hard but well worth it. This project slowly evolved into a heartfelt passion to share with other moms what I've learned about the importance of motherhood and how to make it through daily life as a mom.

Motherhood in today's world is vastly different from the experience our grandmothers and even our mothers faced. We must navigate opportunities and choices that tend to cause confusion about what motherhood is supposed to look like. This book offers an opportunity for moms to explore the emotions that are stirred up in the daily lives of mothers. It also reveals the traps that seek to ensnare moms along the way. I've written this book in such a way that it can be used for self-discovery or in a group setting.

I'm a firm believer in learning from life experiences—my own life experiences and those of others I meet along the way, whether in person, on a blog, or in the pages of a good book. Through my life-experience learning, I've recognized that some people filter their lives through the "Here's what I think" grid. Others filter their lives through the "Here's what God thinks" grid. I was in the former group but am now in the latter.

I'm no scholar or expert, but I have long been a quiet observer, and upon becoming a mom, I started asking other moms a lot of questions and began reading and studying God's Word, seeking to understand Him and His ways. I figured out real fast that raising a child is serious business, as well as hard work.

Once we had children, my husband, Bill, and I moved four times to pursue his career aspirations, and with every move I encountered new moms with familiar issues and challenges that caused me to constantly reevaluate my role as a mom. "Mom" became my professional title, moms became my coworkers, and motherhood became my field of study and evaluation.

Currently I interview both well-known moms and regular moms at *www.momlifetoday.com*, asking them the questions all of us moms ask ourselves daily so that we can gain insight and wisdom from their life experiences! Unwittingly I've become an analyst and gatherer of information regarding the profession of motherhood.

Shaunti Feldhahn, a professional analyst and writer of *For Women Only* as well as a plethora of related books born out of analysis, has referred to me as an authority on motherhood. Who knew? I see myself as a "mom witness," compelled by God to share what He has taught me. God took the passion of my heart and turned it into a desire to reach out to other women to offer help and hope. What started as my personal journey of becoming a mom has evolved into a worldwide outreach to encourage and equip mothers to embrace the title of "Mom" and understand God's unique design for each of us in that role.

Generally speaking, most people lean toward being either aggressive or passive. Life experience and circumstances can alter how far you lean in either direction and can even cause you to lean in the opposite direction at times. In other words, one moment you can be an "I am woman, hear me roar. . . . I can do anything"[1] kind of mom, and the next you can be an "I can't take this anymore. I want to run away" kind of mom.

Why do we get so confused and pulled back and forth between these extremes? Because we get trapped in a certain way of thinking and listen to wrong thoughts and voices that hold us there. It's my prayer that the book you're holding right now will help you escape any trap you might find yourself in. Please know that I've lived through each of the traps described in this book, and I've met other moms mired in these traps as well.

My foray into discovering the wounding nature of the "mom traps" was at times painful—that's why I refer to them as traps. But God does His best work when He frees us from the ties that bind; our job as moms is to be willing to hear, evaluate, and adjust as He prompts us. This book is a personal confession of sorts from a mom who has lived on both sides of the aggressive-passive extreme, but by God's grace has found freedom and joy. My heart's desire is that through the pages of this book, and with God's touch, you will, too.

(And for the record, I had to convince my editor to keep my random snarky comments and extreme exclamatory use within the text of this book. I've always handled tough subjects with a bit of tongue-in-cheek attitude. My snark is not meant to be a bark; it's just the real me.)

CHAPTER 1

My Momlife Journey

I loved being pregnant. Probably because I was told I never would be. The day I first found out I was expecting was glorious. For nearly twelve hours, I was the only one (besides medical staff) who knew.

I had stopped by my gynecologist's office to get some blood work done. My doctor was trying to determine why I didn't ovulate. Every time I stopped by the office in the early morning, I had the all-too-familiar task of peeing in a cup and then getting blood drawn as I chatted with the nurses who were used to seeing my hopeful but constantly dejected face.

As I was gathering up my purse and briefcase to leave, one of the nurses said, "Hey, Tracey, come here a minute." Walking toward her, I could see that she was staring at a small white cylindrical object she was holding in her hand. As I approached her, she held it out to me. I peered into the white plastic orb, cradled between her thumb and forefinger, and saw light blue seeping throughout with a never-before-seen dark-blue dot in the center.

"Does that mean I'm ovulating?" I asked.

She replied, "Uh, no . . . that means you're pregnant."

I stood there for several seconds, staring at the blue dot in her hand, and as I slowly raised my head and looked into her eyes, I honestly feared that she was joking. But her bright eyes and sweet grin, and the soon-to-follow "Congratulations!" she and the other assembled nurses uttered, helped the wonderful truth settle into my quiet, wonder-filled spirit.

Initially I wanted to run from the building screaming, "I'm pregnant! I'm pregnant!" But the greater desire to look into the golden-brown eyes of my husband and tell him before anyone else left me with a secret to keep all to myself. I distinctly remember feeling as if I were floating. I walked to the nearby intercoastal waterway during my lunch hour, spending the entire time talking to and praying for the life in my previously considered "broken" womb. I was filled with gratefulness, wonder, and a deep-felt, excited assurance that all was well.

The thought, *I'm going to be a mom,* constantly swirled through my head.

Toward the end of my workday, I dashed out of the office a bit early in an attempt to beat rush-hour traffic and make a quick stop at a department store to make a special purchase. That weekend was Father's Day, and I had a plan.

When my husband, Bill, got off work, there was a gift waiting for him on the kitchen counter. He picked up the hastily wrapped, flat, rectangular box. "What's this?" he inquired.

"Just a little something I got for you!" I retorted, with a knowing grin.

He opened the box and stared at a tie. "Oh, a tie. That's nice," he said.

I could see he was a bit perplexed at receiving such a random gift. I was staring at him intently, waiting for him to catch on.

"Well, Sunday *is* Father's Day!" I informed him. His eyes met mine, initially with confusion, and then I watched his expression soften, those glowing eyes widen, and a broad, beaming smile take over his tanned, freckled face.

"Are you serious? You're pregnant?" He grabbed me, flung me around, and began laughing as he took in the full knowledge that we were about to be parents. That he was about to be a dad. Grinning, he set me back down on the kitchen floor and looked at me with wonder. Then his face changed. His brow furrowed just a bit, and he whispered, "What are we going to do?"

Bill and I uttered that question over and over during the next eighteen years. (And still do!) We soon learned that parenting isn't for the faint of heart, because parents bear enormous responsibility for the life and future of their children.

Fast-forward sixteen years . . .

$$\circ \quad \circ \quad \circ$$

I blew it. I told myself I wasn't going to make *that* mistake . . . but I did.

You see, when my firstborn started driving, I sort of became a crazy person. I was determined not to be one of those paranoid, controlling parents who must know what her daughter is doing every moment of the day. I told myself to trust her and realize that she needed some space as she learned to spread her wings.

Imagine my surprise when, with this conviction in mind, I watched myself turn into a raving lunatic when my daughter arrived home late one night, not long after getting her license. Sure, she was only a few minutes later than expected. But I knew who she was with, and I knew what they were doing. Yet not hearing from her, combined with the minutes of delay, sent me imagining all manner of calamities most certainly befalling her.

When she walked through the door, I hit the ceiling. Oh yeah, the crazy-mom welcome is sure to strengthen the bond between a parent and a child. Or not.

And the questions—oh *my*—the questions spewing out of my mouth, rapid fire, were enough to make her stand and gawk as if I'd just grown an extra head—a medusa-type one with red eyes, a forked tongue, and snakes writhing and hissing in place of hair!

Okay, I may be exaggerating. But as I've reflected on that event, it's clear I had a meltdown. The kind I swore I would never have. Never say never, I suppose. It was enough to make me wonder, *How do moments like this happen?*

How can a seemingly under-control mom who knows better and wants better (and blogs and speaks and writes about how to be a good mom, for Pete's sake!) manage to slip so far during any given day in her momlife? The truth is that the entire momlife journey is filled with moments of greatness *and* moments of great failure.

If someone would just map out the traps that send us spiraling downward . . . could it prevent us from falling? I've been doing momlife for a while now. I've spent many days hanging out with moms, counseling moms, answering e-mail questions from moms, and I've learned more than a few lessons along the way. I have a story to tell—a real-life story of triumphs and failures. My sometimes-painful journey has led to life change and the realization that I can overcome the traps that seek to ensnare moms. And so, too, can you.

I recognize that I, in my ordinariness, am not alone. Perhaps you have those moments of failure that haunt you, too. Many of us are in various stages of juggling our mom tasks of changing diapers, walking grocery aisles, cooking meals, cleaning (and recleaning), organizing closets, playing games, sitting in carpool lanes, receiving text messages, blogging, tweeting, volunteering, and balancing career goals all while living this all-consuming role of motherhood day after day! If you're anything like me, you may often feel as though you're all alone striving to reach a finish line that requires far too much effort and doesn't offer nearly enough accolades.

Yes, being a mom is wonderful and fulfilling, and it comes with many, many perks. But there are also monumental challenges. There is a reason motherhood is referred to as the hardest and most important job in the world. It is! As with any complex job, it takes a person of unique talent and skill to achieve success. It also takes a person who can appreciate the moments of greatness and learn from the moments of failure.

One of the dangers of having a difficult job is that there can come a time during the heavy lifting when an employee decides it's simply too tough, too much of an assault on self. He or she begins to think, *I'm sick of doing this job! It's time to move on. I quit!* Moving on and quitting, however, are not options for you or me.

Toddlers and Tears

My long-awaited momlife . . . One might envision a picture of tranquillity and a beautifully serene setting. It's late February, and outside the landscape is covered with a blanket of white snow. Inside the cozy two-story home, a young mother is sitting on a warm carpeted stairway, her infant son in her arms and her beautiful, big-brown-eyed, three-year-old daughter resting her head on Mom's shoulder. Lovely.

Well, look again . . . The anticipated love, joy, serenity, and daily fulfillment of motherhood when seen in real-life detail reveals the truth of momlife. In actuality, the baby is screaming his head off, the daughter is crying so much her big brown eyes are bloodshot, and the young mother is also crying uncontrollably as she looks out the window at a blizzard roaring through the little West Virginia town she's just moved to from Palm Beach, Florida.

Welcome to my world as a young mom. At that time I was more than ready to quit being a mom and hand the job over to someone else who would return my kids when they were teenagers.

(Of course, that was before I learned all the issues I'd have to deal with during the teenage years!) The *"I quit"* thought really did skip through my head that day, but I eventually pulled myself together, suited everyone up in winter coats, and trudged through the snow to my pediatrician's office.

There I learned that my daughter had an ear infection, my son had colic, and I had a bad attitude. The joke was on me, for I was the mom who used to think colic was an imaginary infliction conjured up by mothers who just didn't know how to properly take care of a baby.

During those months of caring for my colicky son, I was quite the ray of sunshine around our home. (Do you detect a slight note of sarcasm?) One day Bill was kind enough to relay to me some interesting information he thought was relevant: "Did you know that King Henry the VIII used to demand that his servants wake him every fifteen minutes because the lack of sleep caused him to be especially mean and volatile to his subjects in the kingdom?" (I'm still not sure if he just made that up or spent the afternoon on the Internet looking for an explanation for his wife's attitude.)

As you might have guessed, the night after the diagnosis was a particularly cold night for my husband . . . and not because of the blizzard.

Let's confess, sometimes we as moms fail to see the virtue of sitting on stairways with sick little ones, staying up all night with a colicky baby, changing diaper after diaper, or tending to our children's unending needs. Instead, we fall into the Just-a-Mom trap, thinking, *Do, do, do . . . busy, busy, busy . . . Surely I was put on this earth for something more important than this!*

CHAPTER 2

Just-a-Mom Trap

Is this it . . . really?

I cannot tell you how many times I was asked as a young mom, "So, what do you do?"

In reply, I would hesitantly utter, "I'm just a mom."

I had already realized that my menial life of repetitive tasks—especially when compared to the importance of my previous career—made me "just a mom." I'm sure you can relate to the subtle, and not so subtle, assertion that momlife is an annoying diversion from what a woman's life should really be about. I would like to dispute that assertion.

Whether you're a stay-at-home mom, a career mom, or somewhere in between, momlife actually opens up a whole new aspect of womanhood that should be embraced and explored proudly. However humble many mom tasks might be, we are molding the future, and there is nothing "just" about our role as moms. Can we all agree, right now, to wipe that phrase *just a mom* from the planet?

Professional Woman and Professional Mom

When my husband and I married, we lived in Palm Beach County, Florida. My professional career started on the island of Palm Beach, right there in Donald Trump territory. After graduating from college with a bachelor of arts degree in paralegal science, I easily found a job as a corporate paralegal at the top law firm in South Florida.

As my career developed, I was privileged to travel to some of the finest private golf clubs in the United States, and I ultimately became a membership-and-marketing director at a top-notch private golf club. I definitely got a firsthand look at what the world views as the finer things in life.

After four years of marriage and no baby, I went through some testing and learned that I was unable to get pregnant. I was devastated. Sure, I was pursuing a career and loved it, but motherhood was always part of the plan. Whenever we talked about our future, Bill and I always said, "When we have kids, we will . . ." Suddenly, the dot, dot, dot became a "no kids ever"—period.

I cried. Bill reassured me that it was okay; it wasn't a big deal. But I knew better. From the time we got married, his family had made us perfectly aware of the fact that he was the last male Eyster, and a son was expected. *Well, thanks to me, that's the end of that legacy*, I thought.

We tried Clomid once (it forces ovulation), and it made me ill. We tossed around the thought of jumping through the hoops the doctor suggested to try to force a pregnancy, but in the end we agreed it all sounded way too invasive, and we didn't want to go that route. In my head I considered looking into a surrogate or adoption, but Bill and I ultimately decided to wait and see what the future might hold.

It was easier for my left-brained husband to accept the news. Though the clock was ticking, we chose to ignore it and just live our lives. We carried on our lifestyle as corporate-ladder climbers and went about working, playing, and enjoying the South Florida lifestyle.

We built a large dream home on an exclusive golf course and were on the way to being successful in all the sought-after ways. My husband was on a fast track in management at his job with Pratt and Whitney. He was also pursuing his master's degree by taking night classes, and his future was bright. I traveled a lot and hob-nobbed with the rich and famous. Life as DINKs (dual income, no kids) was good. I convinced myself that not having kids could turn out to be a good thing after all. Bill and I spent our weekdays work-ing and our weekends playing on the beach, on the golf course, and on the tennis court, as well as going out with friends.

After a while, convincing myself that life was great got harder and harder, and the idea of never having children really started to get to me. I had always thought I would be a mom someday, but it really looked as if that wasn't going to happen. My initial resigna-tion to this gradually shifted to frustration and then despair. I was no longer okay with accepting the situation.

Plenty of people in my life tried to reassure me that it would all be fine and that I was lucky to live the life I was living. But I felt so unsettled, as though a promise made to me had been broken. I couldn't believe God would do this to me. In my despair and confusion, I went to the person who I thought had a direct line to God—my grandmother—and I asked her what I should do.

You see, my grandmother was the person in my life who had a very close relationship with God. All my memories of her in-clude a Bible within arm's reach; she was always reading that Bible. On Sundays she would make her family a special "Sunday" dinner. (I can almost smell her delicious fried chicken and those creamy chocolate pies . . . Oops, I digress.)

My grandmother's life modeled what she learned in the Bible.

She always had a kind word for everyone, was always full of joy, and lived her life to serve others—thus Sunday meals for her family at her home. I knew she was the real deal, so I went to her for advice. She suggested I pray and explained to me that God knew the desires of my heart. He would either find a way to give me a child or help me to be content without one.

Bill and I did our best to apply Grandmama's advice, and after many months of prayer, God miraculously blessed us with a pregnancy. Throughout my pregnancy I lived in a constant state of being determined not to be fearful. That's a cloaked way of saying that I was scared to death something was going to go wrong, but I was determined not to give in to the fear.

We had frequent visits to the doctor, who cautioned me to "listen" to my body, which led to my becoming best friends with the book *What to Expect When You're Expecting*. I called my older sister, Shari (who was a mother of two toddlers), weekly to ask questions about what I was feeling and what I should be doing. I wouldn't say I was paranoid, but I was quite intentional about all facets of my burgeoning pregnancy.

I ended up with a borderline case of gestational diabetes, and when my doctor and nutritionist gave me the guidelines for a proper pregnancy diet, I became slightly obsessed with weighing food and eating all the right things. I gave up sodas on the spot and haven't drunk them since! All this listening to my body and following instructions was in full force as we went to our first, and last, Lamaze class. The very next day I went into preterm labor, and at thirty-two weeks of pregnancy, I was ordered to have complete bed rest and was put on a terbutaline pump.

The general manager of the multimillion-dollar private golf course where I worked did not want to hear this news. We were in the throes of a membership drive, as well as major changes at the golf course, and my skill set was much needed. I remember the

GM, a father of five, telling me, "You won't be back," and I assured him I would, because I knew I had to be. Bill and I were mortgaged to the hilt!

As my preterm labor battle continued, I was monitored closely by a home monitor and was relegated to the bed or couch, a cooler of snacks by my side. I received occasional visits from my assistant, who was doing an amazing job of keeping everything at work together while I followed both my doctor's and my husband's orders to do nothing.

We made five emergency trips to the hospital because, for whatever reason, this baby was determined to arrive before her doctor, and parents, wanted her to. The morning I took out of my leg the needle that was pumping my body full of anticontraction medication (following doctor's orders), I went into full labor just prior to thirty-seven weeks. I pushed for hours, but after a sudden drop of the fetal heartbeat, I delivered my sweet baby girl via an emergency C-section, and Bill and I finally became the parents we never thought we would be.

Suddenly our perspectives on life changed—the dream job didn't matter, and the big home and the acquired belongings seemed less important if having them meant sacrificing time spent with my newborn. Still, I loved my job. I didn't really want to leave it, but God kept whispering in my ear, no matter how hard I tried to ignore His voice.

Initially Bill said we didn't have a choice; I had to work. But within weeks he, too, agreed that my staying home was the right thing for our new little family. I was shocked and relieved to realize that once we put pen to paper and formulated a plan, we could afford for me to stay home if we downsized and did some purging. We sold the house, a car, furniture, and everything else that wasn't a necessity, and we purchased a much smaller home in a very different neighborhood.

It was tough, but tough choices are a part of adulthood, and we believed that, for us, this was the right choice. And so I began my new career.

Motherhood, a Hard-Knock Life

In the beginning I approached being a stay-at-home wife and mother as if it were a career, and I decided to use my organizational and communication skills to be diligent and effective at it. We created a budget and stuck to it, ate simple meals, went out less, drove less glamorous cars, and spent lots of time at home enjoying each other and entertaining friends in our home.

I met other moms in our new neighborhood—a nurse whose hours allowed her and her husband to shuffle their schedules so that one of them was always home, a couple of moms who worked part-time, at-home moms and working moms, all struggling to balance everything.

I began to realize that there are options when you become a mom. You just have to have the tenacity to explore what is best for your own family and then be brave enough to make it happen. I spent the early years of motherhood accepting my role as important and understanding that what was best for my child was learning to see myself as a mom first.

Even though I was no longer a professional, I still had a desire to use my skills and talents, and I did by serving in my church and community. I also found ways to make a little bit of money—I learned that many opportunities were out there for making some extra money, and many people were willing to find ways to work with the needs of a mom's schedule.

My mom schedule got a bit more crowded when another miracle occurred and God blessed us with the birth of a son. Even though that pregnancy went a bit smoother, I still ended up on bed rest, and at thirty-six weeks, my son decided it was time to make an early appearance! Around that same time, we moved to West Virginia. Being deposited in a new state, having a baby and a toddler, and knowing no one, I recognized that I was very lonely, my at-home career was *not* glamorous, and—quite frankly—on most occasions all that I did went unnoticed.

My belief in the extreme importance of my role as a full-time mom was challenged when new acquaintances I was meeting hit me with the question, " You're a stay-at-home mom . . . So what do you do all day?" It's the age-old question every stay-at-home mom would like to shove right back into the mouth of anyone who asks it in a derogatory way.

"Well . . . I eat bonbons and paint my toenails, of course! What do you do in that office all day? Trade jokes; take long, leisurely lunches; and chat on Twitter?" Of course, both are far from the truth. (I'm assuming.)

Okay, I'll tell you what we do as moms. We prepare all the meals. Clean everything. Wash everything. Read to the little ones. Play with the little ones. Pick up after the little ones. Referee the little ones. Shop for everything, with the little ones in tow. I could go on, but I think you get the message. Actually I think you *live* the message.

It's not just stay-at-home moms who face the aggravation of the unglamorous role of motherhood. Moms with careers feel it too, because they do everything a stay-at-home mom does once they hit the door after a long day's work outside the home.

And don't even get me started on the life of a single mom! Two of my best friends are doing it alone—raising children and working full-time. I see firsthand how physically and emotionally exhausted they feel from the constant demands of motherhood. Their options for maintaining balance require a fortitude that I don't think I could manage.

What I came to recognize early on in my parenting journey is this: The major frustration for all moms is that the same thankless, unending parade of duties must be done day after day. Even enjoyable activities wear on you when you repeat them often enough.

How could something I prayed so long for, something I left my career for, become drudgery? But isn't that true of most jobs, once you've been at it for a while? It takes a rocket scientist to get tired of being a rocket scientist. I wanted to be a mother, I prayed to be a mother, but being just a mom, at times, was unexciting, monotonous, and thankless.

I was beginning to feel that motherhood was unimportant, and in filling that role, I was becoming an overlooked nobody. What's with that voice in our heads that constantly tells us we don't matter . . . especially when we're being the mom? We devalue ourselves in our own minds. Or do we? Is something besides our own self-talk gnawing at us?

In most every fairy tale—whether classic or modern—we see a battle of good versus evil. We see this in today's popular epic movies as well. These stories reflect real life, for the Bible tells us that we, as humans, face an evil enemy every day. It describes him in 1 Peter 5:8: "Your enemy the devil prowls around like a roaring lion looking for someone to devour."

One of my favorite fictional books is C. S. Lewis's *The Screwtape Letters*, because it so creatively points out the ways the Enemy tries to thwart God's plan for us through the ordinariness of everyday life. This book is a series of letters a demon named Screwtape writes to his nephew Wormwood, giving him advice on how to win over the "creature" (human) he is trying to turn away from God:

You see, it is so hard for these creatures to persevere. The routine of adversity, the gradual decay of youthful loves and youthful hopes, the quiet despair (hardly felt as pain) of ever overcoming the chronic temptations with which we have again and again defeated them, the drabness which we create in their lives and the inarticulate resentment with which we teach them to respond to it—all this provides admirable opportunities of wearing out a soul by attrition.[1]

Mom, are you feeling worn out? Do you feel resentful? Are you feeling trapped in the mundane tasks of your momlife? I get it! I've been there, especially when I was a mom of young ones. I, too, struggled with the Just-a-Mom trap!

I constantly talk to and read letters from moms who struggle with this recurring thought. It seems as though being a mom is wearing them out. It's high time you drown out the whispers of this mom lie with a healthy dose of mom truth about just how important your momlife really is, and why perseverance in your role as a mom is crucial for you and your children.

The importance of gaining a true understanding of why you are more than just a mom is pivotal, because if you don't, you'll become overwhelmed and burdened by negative self-talk, and end up sitting on a stairway crying and feeling like a total failure. When your thoughts are thumping loudly with, *I'm just a mom, and I can't even do that well*, the trap has a vicelike grip on you that can lead to utter despair.

The good news is that if that's where you are now, you don't have to stay there.

Powerful Motherhood and Welcoming Wisdom

Have you ever noticed that any time you make up your mind to "get after" something, you're a force to be reckoned with? Were you an athlete in high school? As a college student, did you have to work hard to make the grades? Did you play an instrument in the band? Were you on the debate team? Were you an honor student? You name it, whatever it was, I bet there was something you were really good at.

Did you know that according to some studies, more than 40 percent of college students drop out during their freshman year?[2] Popular wisdom teaches that the high dropout rate is because those students didn't have a plan, or didn't stick to their plan. Your successes in life are achieved by embracing various roles as challenges, working hard, and recognizing setbacks as ways to adjust and improve, not as times to give in to feelings of defeat.

I have my pom-poms at the ready. You can do it, Mom! Grasp the truth that you are important, and that approaching each day with a can-do attitude and suiting up for the challenge will go a long way in helping you find victory in your momlife.

Practically, that means you need to have a plan that includes the following:

1. Have a "mom uniform." In other words, wear clothes daily that make you feel cute! (Let's face it, it matters!)
2. Create a schedule that helps you stay on track, allowing "white space" for the unexpected.
3. Eat breakfast, lunch, and dinner. Skipped meals means a grouchy mom.
4. When the kids are napping, at practice, or working on homework, take a nap or do something that relaxes you while they're occupied.
5. Every day must include some form of physical activity for you and your children. It's possible even during bad weather. When all else fails, two basic options are always available: walking or dancing.
6. Smile, smile, smile, giggle, giggle, giggle. Yes, I'm serious. Whether it's funny books, funny tapes, funny jokes, or funny faces, laughter breeds a home full of good cheer.

7. Reserve quiet time for you and your children. At first it may need to be forced, but once you've cultivated the habit in your family, it becomes a need. Read the Bible, enjoy a book, journal, draw, think, dream—no media, just peace. Even if initially it's just for fifteen minutes, start somewhere and make it happen.

I'm rooting for you, Mom! Have you ever backed down from something you weren't so good at doing? That first college paper you wrote may have been a marked-up mess, but you didn't start hiring someone else to write your papers (at least I hope not); you did the work it took, met with the professor, asked the brainiac upperclassman down the hall for help, did more research, pulled all-nighters. You did what it took to be successful.

Notice a common thread in where the aforementioned paper-writing-challenged student found assistance? Did she sit in the stairwell and cry? Did she lock herself up in her room and will herself to write a better paper? Negative. She reached outside of herself and asked others for help. She sought out the older and wiser professor.

You need to find that empty-nest mom—the been-there-done-that upperclassman. Do you have a neighbor or a friend from church with children older than yours? A friend can make all the difference. (We'll talk about this more in our Mirror Mom chapter.) Consider reaching out to other moms online. Come visit my group of amazing friends at *www.momlifetoday.com*. You, too, can do what it takes to know that you are more than just a mom.

I've found that many of us set our expectations too high; we expect ourselves to naturally figure out this being-a-mom thing. We all need help, and it's a good thing when we go to others for assistance and advice.

Rather than viewing momlife as a "less than" choice, I chose to shift perspectives. I decided that "it's not about what I'm not doing, but about what I *am* doing." I reminded myself that I'm blessed to have children—there are women whose arms ache to hold and love a child every day.

When I would feel overwhelmed by the chaos that was staring me in the face at home, I would think of those who have no home. When I was frustrated at the thought of dragging myself out of bed and starting the "same day" all over again, I would ponder, *Did my husband think the same thing this morning? He got up and got going, so I must do the same.*

Having a heart of gratitude is essential in the life of a mom, and practicing gratitude transforms our hearts from being self-focused to being God-focused. That focus is a wonderful attribute to pass along to our children; grateful children are contented no matter their circumstances.

What I've come to understand time after time is that my role as a mother—and all that goes with it in creating a safe, happy home where my family can thrive—is a good thing. When you pull back to view the whole of your life and look at the big picture, wherever

mom truth ○

The changes I saw in my body as a result of being pregnant now seem to pale in comparison to the changes I've seen in my personality as I have embraced motherhood. The ability to truly understand the pressures of motherhood cannot be understood unless you are a mother. You're not alone in this, Mom! Your value as a mother is unsurpassed. You haven't lost yourself; you've found who you were destined to become. You've been given lives to mold and an opportunity to prepare your children for the future. There is nothing "just a mom" about you.

you are right now, it's just a season of your life. A season that may seem like an eternity while you're in the middle of it, but in actuality is very brief. (We'll go a little deeper with this in our Tomorrow Mom chapter.)

I have an amazing, young military-wife mom friend I would like to introduce you to. Her name is Nicole, and you can meet her right now at *www.lifesabatch.com*. Once your mouth stops watering, ruminate on the fact that making cookies that look like works of art is the method Nicole uses to keep herself feeling a bit sassy, happy, and upbeat! She isn't just a mom; she's a *great* mom who loves to bake some magnificent cookies and who shares her gift with others. She found an outlet for her creativity, and believe me, this is so important.

Make a list of the things you like to do that bring you joy! Not work stuff . . . fun stuff! If you aren't sure what those things are, ask yourself, "What did I like to do before I had children?" Being a mom is hard work, and we know that all work and no play leads to a lousy attitude about being a mom. I'm just sayin' we need to learn to persevere and find ways to remain joyful in our everyday-mom lives, because motherhood is essential.

The Message Bible says it well in 2 Corinthians 4:1: "Since God has so generously let us in on what he is doing, we're not about to throw up our hands and walk off the job just because we run into occasional hard times." Therefore, Mom, don't "throw up your hands and walk off the job"; find something for those hands to do in the midst of your momlife that will keep your joy tank filled.

If you want to make time for fun but feel you can't because of your children, I encourage you to work out a system with a friend or family member where you trade childcare. My friend Tawnya and I recognized our need to have time to do things outside of mothering, so we worked out a regular schedule where we would take turns caring for each other's children. I'll bet there's another mom who would welcome the opportunity to do some childcare swapping with you. It wouldn't hurt to ask!

Take a look at your schedule. Where could you fit in time to pursue something that brings you joy? I know lots of online moms who blog and connect with like-minded moms after the kids go to bed. I have a friend who jogs early in the morning before her kids awaken, and another friend who takes an art class one night a week.

If you can find even a bit of time to do what fills your tank, it will help you be more content in whatever season of life you're in. I encourage you to enjoy your daily momlife and remember to giggle more!

Just-a-Mom-Trap Quiz

Please read the following statements and rate yourself on a scale from one (strongly agree) to five (strongly disagree). Then answer the corresponding questions or follow the instructions. If you're reading this book with a group, these questions can serve as discussion starters. Share as you feel comfortable.

1. I find value in being a mom. _____

   Why do you agree or disagree with this statement?

2. I will make an effort to change any resentful thoughts I have about my momlife. _____

   List some practical steps you will take to recognize motherhood as a gift and calling, more than "just a mom."

3. I recognize that each stage of motherhood is a season, and I'm able to enjoy each season as a mom. _____

List the seasons you've been through to date and the positives of each one.

4. I approach my daily mom duties with a good attitude. _____

   Describe three times this week when you chose a good attitude and three times when you chose a bad attitude.

5. I find joy in interests and/or hobbies outside of motherhood. _____

   List those interests you currently enjoy or those you would like to start doing.

Scoring Chart

5–8 = You know who you are, and you place great value in being a mom.

9–12 = You know who you are, but being a mom is getting to you a bit.

13–16 = You are trying to be happy as a mom, but your thought life is a problem.

17–20 = You are dangerously close to being trapped; you need to change course.

21–25 = You see yourself as just a mom, and you are desperate for rescue. This chapter is for you! And I hope you'll keep reading—more help and hope are coming your way! If you need further encouragement or advice, visit me at my blog *www.bethemom.com*. Let's connect!

Next Up . . .

If you've never taken the time to read Proverbs 31:10-31 (or even if it's just been awhile since you've read it), I suggest you stop here and do so. By reading those passages, you'll understand why the phrase "just a mom" is far from accurate.

You are more than just a mom. You are the mom of _____ _____ (insert your children's names here), and your children are a gift. Let me encourage you: Though there are traps ahead, they're avoidable, including the trap that I like to refer to as the Me Mom trap. Read on, sister friend!

CHAPTER 3

Me Mom Trap

It's my way or else, people!

Even though a few different things may come to your mind when you hear the Me Mom trap described, we're going to stick to how it manifests itself in the confines of running our households. We can giggle nervously and roll our eyes playfully and refer to ourselves in the acceptable terminology frequently used: "I'm a bit of a control freak." Or I can look at you ink to eye (lean into the book) and confront you with the possibility that you might be in the Me Mom trap.

Most of us have the capacity to be trapped at one time or another in any given mom trap, and we spend time with other moms whose traps may be different from ours. That's why exploring, understanding, and obtaining knowledge on how to break free from them is important. I've spent some time in the Me Mom trap, still visit it on occasion, and with a heart of understanding and compassion, would like to explore with you the question, "What's up with my need to control?"

The Me Mom trap is rooted in pride. Let me share how pride comes into play here. For me, learning that the world didn't revolve around me and my wants and needs was painful but ultimately led to relief and freedom.

When I was caught in this Me Mom trap, I thought that everyone around me needed to meet my expectations, and when they didn't, it affected my ability to have joy. It even made me impossible to live with . . . Oh yeah, I went *there*.

Avoiding the Me Mom trap is an ongoing responsibility for me. Basically, I can be ugly. I'm from the South; that's how we Southerners describe someone who isn't nice. Sometimes my ugliness is blatant and I just lash out; at other times I use sarcasm and manipulation to elicit guilt. Yes, even after writing this book, I can still make it all about me. But I've learned to recognize when it has happened and then to seek forgiveness and reconciliation—but honestly, sometimes I don't even do that well. Case in point . . .

I was a bit stretched. There were too many things to get done and not enough time to do it all—a sure setup for "ugly" to occur. I know you can relate. Anyway, I had my tasks to complete, and my children had theirs. I was working hard . . . and they were goofing off. Shocking, right?

I snapped.

It went something like this: "I am so sick of always being the one who has to do everything! I'm in here making dinner, all the while assuming that you two are doing your chores, and instead, you're playing around and goofing off! Those chores should have been done a long time ago. I'm sick of this!"

I got stares and silence; then my son said, "I'm sorry, Mom, I'll do better."

With that I stomped away. I was back in the kitchen, scurrying around, and as my blood pressure began to settle, I heard that still small voice say, *That didn't go well, did it? What did you just teach them to do when someone doesn't live up to their expectations? Rant like a lunatic and vent your frustration on someone smaller than you.*

So after some time praying and contemplating, I went back to both of them and apologized. This was my apology: "I am so sorry I raised my voice at you . . . BUT it's very disappointing to me when you don't do the things I ask you to do. We all have to do our part around here; this family is a team."

There it is—my big "BUT." That big BUT shouldn't have been there. A true apology doesn't include a big BUT. I felt convicted to apologize for my actions, not make an excuse for them by placing a big BUT on the end! (Do you get the word picture here, friends? That's some motivation!)

I never stopped to consider that my son had had a rough day at school, and talking to and joking with his sister was actually helping him. They knew what was required and what the consequences would be if their chores weren't done. My lashing out at them was more about my issues at that moment than theirs. I was feeling stretched and pushed, and I took it out on them.

When we moms stomp around the house and mutter words that include lots of "I's," it's time to recognize that the Me Mom trap has been sprung.

The Pursuit of Perfection

As a mother, you've seen self-absorption in your children from the time they were born. When a baby doesn't get her way because she's hungry, she cries. When a toddler doesn't get his way because he doesn't want to take a nap (even though he needs one), he whines.

When a school-age child doesn't want to go to school one day, that child will pout or lash out in anger, or both. When a teenager doesn't want to leave the football game after-party because she's having too much fun, she decides to disobey her parents, set her own rules, and ignore her curfew. Do you see a pattern here?

Each of these children has the "meism" disease we all know as selfishness—my wants, my needs, my fulfillment, my way. Could it be that inherently we all drift toward wanting things our way? We, as moms (and wives), can be guilty of this same meism. And I say "we" because including you in this realization softens the pain a bit for me, and if this is a trap you've found yourself in, I hope it softens your pain, too.

At times my head fills with thoughts like these: *I want a clean house every moment. How dare those children of mine not live up to my expectations of cleanliness! I want every family member seated at the table at precisely 6:30 PM so we can enjoy a family meal together. I want to watch my show, I want to go out to eat, I want the leaky toilet fixed—now. I want obedient, "perfect" children. I want a husband devoted to my needs every moment of every day, and I want him to figure out what those needs are without me even having to tell him.*

When the "I" thoughts start flying through my head, the "I" words are usually not far behind. Proverbs 14:1 tells us, "The wise woman builds her house, but with her own hands [and mouth] the foolish one tears hers down." I've learned through doing it wrong often enough that I need to release my grip on what I want and how I want things done.

I want my children to be productive, and I want a home that is run efficiently, but I'm not raising little robots. I am raising uniquely designed children who thrive best when they're encouraged in big ways. The "little engine that could" got there because he believed in himself, not because he was following strict orders. I want my children to believe in themselves and to know that I also believe in them.

It's a well-known fact in the business world that employees thrive when they're allowed to do their jobs without feeling stifled or hovered over. Have you ever heard of the pot-making principle? It's a business principle my husband shared with me. Two groups of people were asked to make the perfect pot. One group was told they could only make one pot, but it better be perfect. The other group was told they could do whatever they wanted, but the end result must also be perfect.

The first group met and discussed and thought about and labored over their one perfect pot. The second group started making pots, discovering what worked and what didn't and tossing failed pots aside as they improved the process. In the end, the second group had a far superior pot because they had learned how to make a better pot by trial and error.

Your children will learn to do everything better by trial and error. Don't expect more than they can deliver, and be mindful to encourage them toward improvement. Avoid discouraging them with a "You don't measure up" message, which will lead to lack of confidence. This is the mom trap that probably holds the greatest danger for your children—a danger that has been referred to as performance-based love.

I do realize there are two schools of thought on this: "Do it right" or "Do your best." My experience has taught me that for younger children who are learning, the "Do it right" message will definitely get it done, but the "Do your best" message will get your children to *want* to accomplish the task in front of them.

A mother once told me that if her children's beds weren't made up exactly the way she wanted them to be, her kids had to do them over and over until they were right. She went on to proudly declare that there was only one way to fold a towel: her way. And the towels had to be done perfectly or redone. I was thinking, *Really? That's what you want to teach your children? God has given you children so that they'll know how to make a bed and fold a towel . . . your way?*

There's a difference between teaching children responsibility and a good work ethic and forcing them to snap to attention at your every command. I fear the latter method lacks love, nurturing, and encouragement. We all want to guide our children toward responsibility; we just need to remember that making pots with a positive attitude, even while making mistakes, leads to success in the long run. Our words and directives that spur on the pot making need to encourage and lift up our children. Remember that the next time you hear controlling utterances coming out of your mouth, because there is no pause or delete button when it comes to life.

O   O   O

So, how do you yank yourself out of the Me Mom trap? When you start hearing (aloud or in your head) the word *I* over and over again, replace the "I's" with the thought, *Why am I seeking control here? It's not about me,* and ask God to reveal how the situation could become a teaching moment.

My husband is a child of divorce, and when his mother remarried, there was tension in the home. Bill's grades were less than stellar, and his stepfather, Al, was an academician, a college professor. His nature was to demand academic excellence, but he made a very wise decision when he asked Bill's mother, "Do you want me to force Bill to make good grades, or do you want peace in our home?" She chose peace.

As a result, Bill and his stepfather have a strong, loving relationship. And Bill ended up with decent grades. With love and understanding, Al encouraged Bill to improve, but he didn't make their home a battlefield and force the issue. I see that as wisdom based on the circumstances—something parents need to consider when deciding what the nonnegotiables and the not-worth-fighting-over issues are in their own homes. Slowly, through Al's encouragement, Bill became a better student and went on to get stellar grades in college and earn an MBA.

As moms, when we're trying to teach our children responsibility and a good work ethic, it's important that our focus be on helping them improve in the task at hand, not getting things done our way. If our demands and rules leave no room for teaching, improvement, and encouragement, an ever-widening gap will form between us and our children. Teaching our children with love and understanding should be our goal.

Teach Your Children Well

I'm convinced that our children learn how to react to their world through everyday life in the home. They model behavior they learn from us. It's just common sense that our children will learn from our actions and reactions. Because of this, and since we all have the tendency to want things our way, recognizing the Me Mom trap and learning to avoid it will serve you and your children well. The following steps can help:

1. Avoid thinking and speaking "I" thoughts, but when you do have those moments, examine your motives. Are they leaving opportunity for teaching your children?
2. Determine what your children are capable of, and don't expect more than they can accomplish.
3. Challenge your children toward more responsibility, new activities, and chores. But rather than chastising them when something isn't done "just right," encourage and embolden them, which will foster improvement.
4. Don't base your personal self-worth on the condition of your home. Your priority isn't your home; it is the hearts and souls of the people in your home.
5. If you have unspoken frustrations while at home, stop and recognize that those frustrations shouldn't be taken out on your children. Discuss them with your spouse, call a friend, journal, or make a list and determine how to resolve the issue or live with it without giving in to frustration.

6. Decide what you consider the nonnegotiables for a smooth-running home. Come up with a plan for getting those accomplished regularly; then place the negotiables on a when-we-have-extra-time list and let them wait.

7. Cut yourself, and those around you, some slack. No one on their deathbed ever said, "Oh no, my baseboards need cleaning."

When it comes to teaching children responsibilities around the home, I know moms who use chore charts, complete with rewards. You can set aside one day a week for chores or space things out by assigning one chore a day.

The way we tackled the get-it-all-done monster in our home was by writing down on slips of paper all the chores that needed to be done weekly and then placing those slips of paper in a jar. We'd each draw a chore—this kept family members from getting burned-out on certain chores. Two of the slips of paper in the jar were "mom's choice" and "kid's choice," and there was also a list of "someday chores" that were optional. We even had a "no chore" slip, just to keep things interesting. If you drew one of those, you got to talk a little smack—just to be playful!

I know of one woman who had a great need for order, but her teenage daughter had a need for creativity, so they came up with a brilliant solution. The teen kept all her clothes in two dressers, and her closet was turned into an area she could do whatever she wanted with—and it ended up being a jumbled, artistic, creative mess. But out of sight meant out of Mom's mind; they found a compromise and they were both happy.

The main principle here is to use a system that clarifies your expectations and keeps things a bit lighthearted. Part of your children's nature is to be playful, so go with their natural bent as they learn responsibility! You want to set your children up for success. One way to do this is to equip them to step up to a challenge and thereby enjoy a feeling of accomplishment. As a result, you will all enjoy the happiness of being part of a family that works together.

How we treat one another in the home influences how our children will someday treat their roommates, their coworkers, their future spouses, and their own children.

My Way

If you've mastered the art of not being too demanding of your children, I would like to give you a big hug and offer you hope that your children will end up with a perfect pot one day! My daughter can make a bathroom sparkle! My son's room can look picture perfect!

Keep reading, though, because there is another side to this trap we need to explore too. Be careful not to cross over to the easy way out of the Me Mom trap, which has its own set of snares. Your answer to this question can reveal whether you're doing this: Do you do most everything for your children to prevent conflict and make things easier? If you're taking the easy way out, not only are you robbing your children of teachable moments, but you may also have an underlying need for control that causes you to demand too much from yourself. I know this from personal experience. I had that "I'll just do it myself so it's done right" approach early on in my mothering.

I used to take such pride in opening the linen closet and observing a perfectly stacked set of towels and washcloths. Such an observation would fill me with a sense of order and an assurance that all was well within my household because the linen closet was neat and tidy. (I see a psychology lesson in that warped logic.)

My day was filled with providing, serving, and preparing, while the little ones ripped, roared, and had fun. As an involved mom, I've spent my fair share of time on the floor, right in the middle of all the fun. But when it came to chores around the house and providing for our daily needs, it was just easier, faster, and more efficient for me to do it myself.

Okay, confession time. Actually, it was better to do it myself because then it would be done right. The problem was that I worked myself ragged in my pursuit of things being done right! Anyone else suffer from this problem?

When we choose to do tasks our children could be doing, just to make sure they're done "right," we are missing the opportunity to teach our children capability and responsibility. We should be training our children to do for themselves and serve others. The only way your child will ever be able to make a good peanut butter and jelly sandwich is to make two dozen of them. Sure, the first twenty-three will be lumpy, and your countertop will be laden with crumbs and jelly blobs, but hey, before you know it, you'll have a capable and skilled helper when you're serving lunch to neighborhood playmates.

I figured out the principle of having my young children "help" me with the daily tasks around the house one day while I was folding laundry. I decided that we would fold together and that I would turn the task into a time of prayer. We discussed that we would say a special prayer for the person whose laundry we were folding. Inspired idea, right? Only one problem—in the process of this intended sweet time of prayer, I was becoming a basket case.

As I sat there, systematically rolling socks into perfect little balls, I noticed that my daughter wasn't properly folding Daddy's T-shirts, and they were becoming all askew. That caused me to feel a bit anxious. I then swiveled around just in time to see my son take a clean towel, lay it on the floor, and start folding. Can you believe that? Clean towels on the floor—I was horrified!

To make his hideous infraction even more grievous, he was tossing one "folded" towel upon another, and they were getting all bunched up, not properly aligned. I know, isn't that just awful? My son then proceeded to pick up his large stack of disheveled towels and disappear. When he returned, he was all excited, grabbed me by the hand, and asked me to come look.

We trotted down the hallway together to the linen closet. And before my eyes, in my normally pristine linen closet, was the worst mess of "folded" towels I had ever seen. I was aghast. I was about to snatch them out of the closet and redo them "right." But when I looked down at my son to explain his mistake, I froze. The look of delight and accomplishment on his sweet little face was precious.

That's when it hit me: It's my job to teach him, with encouragement and patience, how to fold towels, how to share with his sister, have a quiet time, respectfully talk to others, and so much more. As his primary teacher, I would accomplish none of that if I was controlling and wanted everything done my way and "perfect." This little boy who was eager to help me and worked so diligently to accomplish the task at hand deserved a good cheering, not a controlling mother's chastising.

Colossians 3:21 came to mind: "Do not embitter your children, or they will become discouraged." And then Ephesians 6:4: "Do not exasperate your children; instead, bring them up in the training and instruction of the Lord."

The Lord redirected my response to that less-than-perfect linen closet. My son beamed happily as he watched me do a little dance of joy while clapping excitedly. I enthusiastically gave him a high five and told him he did a great job. Those words of encouragement caused him to want to help in other ways and do his best. If I had used words of condemnation, I'm guessing he wouldn't have been at all interested in being my little helper.

That day I learned a valuable lesson: It's more important to work *with* my children to complete household chores than it is to get everything done "right." Interestingly, I also learned that in the long run, as my children do chores and I playfully guide them toward improvement in completing certain tasks, the better they get at doing those tasks.

I remember the first carrot cake I made as a newlywed; it *totally* bombed, but my husband didn't lash out at me for messing up the cake. If he had, that would have ended my cake-baking career. And then my "world-famous" chocolate-chocolate-chocolate cake never would have been invented—and that would have been a real crime!

Not only did my kids slowly improve in their chore-completion skills; they also began to enjoy our time of "Chores and Prayers," and it has evolved into "Chores, Praise, and Prayers," because as they've grown older, we've added the element of some seriously loud praise music!

I realize now that the days of perfect linen closets will return far too soon, since my children are growing up fast, and way before I'm ready for it, they will be leaving the nest. Who knows, once they're out of the house, I may even place my towels in the linen closet all askew, in spite of myself, as I lift up a prayer for my children.

mom truth

The order and structure I demanded in my home was a counterfeit attempt to feel peace and contentment. Seeking to control our surroundings by making unnecessary demands on our children or ourselves will disrupt the love in our homes. You are to be your child's gentle and encouraging teacher. You won't find personal happiness in taking order and rules to an extreme, but you and your children will flourish when you replace the Me Mom attitude with a heart of grace.

If you find yourself trapped in the "I want this done my way" Me Mom trap, let me suggest recognizing that most things can be done more than one way!

The Promise

Are you aware that only one of the Ten Commandments comes with a promise? Deuteronomy 5:16 says, "Honor your father and your mother, as the LORD your God has commanded you, so that you may live long and that it may go well with you."

As you reflect on this commandment, recognize that the way you train up and teach your children affects the way they react to you—and the world around them. If you want this promised life blessing for your children, be mindful of what you teach in your home and how you teach it.

If at times you do have moments you regret because you've spoken or acted in a manner that was too harsh, go to your children and apologize—and take it from me, leave the big BUT out of the apology! I also need you to hear me clearly on this point: Don't be too hard on yourself. We all have those moments of regret, but God's grace can cover them.

Say it aloud with me now: "I will mess up as a mom at times, but I will not ruin my children in the process." Let me assure you that I have a list, a *long* list, of my epic-fail moments that tumble through my ponytail-coiffed head. I've learned that when we try our best but have those epic-fail moments, God has an amazing way of magnifying the sweetness of the day and burying the uglies. He is so gracious like that.

Mom, stop beating yourself up over your mistakes and the bad days, and instead focus on the moments of sweetness and the good days. Remember the fear you had when you were first handed your newborn? Like me, you may have wondered if you were going to physically harm her as you fumbled with her tininess. But she never broke, did she? If you're trying to do your very best, she won't break. Every day is an opportunity to start fresh, and children are forgiving. Remember, they thrive when they're challenged by a joy-filled mom!

Me-Mom-Trap Quiz

Please read the following statements and rate yourself on a scale from one (strongly agree) to five (strongly disagree). Then answer the corresponding questions or follow the instructions.

1. I get that we all have a tendency, at times, to struggle with "me-ism", but I manage pretty well to recognize it and alter my course.

    List a few times this week when you suffered from "meism."

2. I am able to apologize to my children when I have a meism moment. _____

    Describe a time when you did apologize to your children, and/or a time when you should have.

3. I recognize that I need to teach my children, not "command" them. _____

List two areas you know you need to approach differently.

4. I approach my daily mom duties as a teacher. _____

   List an area where you know you have taught your children well.

5. My actions toward my children make it easy for them to honor me and receive God's blessing. _____

   Why is it important for you to teach your children to honor you? (Read Deuteronomy 5:16.)

Scoring Chart

5–8 = You know your actions affect your children, and you are working to be a teaching mom.

9–12 = You know your actions affect your children, but you are struggling with wanting things your way.

13–16 = You are trying to be a teaching mom, but wanting things your way is a problem.

17–20 = You are dangerously close to being trapped; you need to change course.

21–25 = You are in the Me Mom trap, and you are desperate for rescue.

Pray this prayer: Father, help me to model serving You for my children, _____ (place children's names here), teaching them how to serve and honor others so that they have every opportunity to follow the commandment "Honor your father and your mother, as the LORD your God has commanded you, so that you may live long and that it may go well with you" (Deuteronomy 5:16) and receive the promised blessing.

Next Up . . .

A close cousin to the Me Mom trap is the trap I continually find myself in, and I am totally ashamed to admit it. I think I could be the poster mom for the Martyr Mom trap, and in an act of complete humility (and extreme embarrassment), I am going to lay it all out in black and white in the next chapter.

CHAPTER 4

Martyr Mom Trap

Another cold meal for me.

One of my daughter's favorite books when she was very young was a Winnie-the-Pooh book. I remember that when I read it to her, she would point at Eeyore and say, "So sad." Even a toddler could see by the way that old donkey was drawn that he was one miserable mammal.

If your life were a children's book, what would the illustrations in your story reveal about you to a perceptive child? You may not realize it, but I'm guessing there are times when your countenance reveals more than you would like it to.

To this day, when I encounter a particularly downtrodden individual, I sort of make it my mission during my time with that person to cheer her up and love on her a little bit. I must admit, I sometimes think, *There's an Eeyore*. If she's a mom, I wonder, *Is she an Eeyore who is entangled in the Martyr Mom trap?* I can usually spot her easily, because I used to look at her every day—she lived in my purse . . . in my powder compact.

In my wonderfulness of giving full attention to my family, I began to neglect myself. Oh yeah, I looked pitiful. I acted pitiful. "Woe is me. I'm sacrificing my own well-being and happiness for the good of my family. Someone pat me on the back, shake your head in admiration, and build a statue in my honor."

It's humbling when those who know you best say the simplest things that hold a mirror (a full-length one at that) in front of you and reveal what you've become. That mirror bearer was my wonderful little brother, Tim. He and I have always been especially close, and in one of my "admire me for my sacrifice" Martyr Mom moments, I said to him, "I'm so busy caring for my family and doing everything for them that I just have no time for myself. I think I'm starting to gain too much weight."

Most innocently, and not one bit mean-spirited, he said to me, "No, you're just getting fluffy." Fluffy . . . *fluffy*? He may as well have slapped me across the face, that word stung so much. It sounded just awful as it rolled around in my head and settled on my tongue, and I repeated it over and over for the next few weeks. *Fluffy* denotes inactivity, laziness, and lack of movement.

Well, actually that was pretty accurate. I had become fluffy—fluffy body, fluffy attitude, and fluffy spiritual growth. I went through a period when I wasn't being the wife I was supposed to be, the mom I was supposed to be, or the child of God I was supposed to be. I was in the Martyr Mom trap.

I had turned full circle and gone from it being all about me to it being so not about me that I copped a "poor pitiful me" attitude. I think I subconsciously allowed my misery to manifest itself in my attitude and appearance. I had sort of given up on myself and wanted to make sure it was obvious to the entire world that I had done just that.

Through the years, I have learned I'm not alone. Once, while I was facilitating a study with a small group of moms, I shared this part of my past, and the room was filled with nodding heads. Afterward, two different ladies came up to me crying, saying that for the first time they had heard themselves described.

I think this is a mom trap that few women are willing to admit to, because it's so unattractive and embarrassing to admit such shortcomings. I continually hear from moms who become overwhelmed and give up, or decide they just don't care anymore. They painfully admit that they shut down and wear their weariness in their countenance.

If this describes you, take heart, Mom! The beauty of revelation is that you are then able to overcome. The beauty of sharing my battle in that small group and here with you is that if you, or a friend of yours, is trapped in the martyrdom slump, there is a way out. You can escape! You can break out of the Martyr Mom trap if you resolve to engage in a few simple daily practices that uplift you:

1. Admit you have an Eeyore attitude and resolve to improve your countenance; just naming it and working to change it provides momentum toward change.
2. Tell a friend that you're striving to live with a more positive attitude, and ask her to keep you accountable.
3. Focus daily on five things you will get accomplished that day—and get after them! (Start with small things to ensure success and then up the ante!)
4. Find music that inspires you and uplifts you . . . and turn it up loud!
5. Be up on your feet more than you're sitting or lying down.
6. Find a way each week to serve others. Focusing on the needs of others will infuse you with energy and purpose.
7. Tell yourself you can do this. Positive self-talk is so important.

After that "fluffy" comment from my brother, I grappled with what to do to become Tracey again, not this sad little creature who had given in to being overwhelmed by motherhood. I decided I would pray for the desire and motivation to get up off my "nevermind" and get moving again. I pulled out my dusty Bible and started reading it again . . . a little bit. I saw some improvement, but not much.

I took the aforementioned steps to pull myself up out of the doldrums, including getting up at a set time every day and reinstituting the guidelines I had put in place to get out of the Just-a-Mom trap. Remember? Dressing cute, white space on the calendar, giggling—all that good stuff. I also received a very important revelation that tied directly into how my attitude was affecting my mothering habits.

The revelation came one day as I sat watching my children play instead of playing with them. When my children were toddlers, I was exhausted all the time—let's face it, all moms of toddlers are exhausted all the time. I remember too well that every day was the same: a blur of cleaning, cooking, helping, fixing, teaching, correcting, organizing, planning, inviting, wiping, reading, soothing, redoing, over and over and over again.

In my exhausted state, I would take my children outside and set them up in the yard to play. There would be a nice little pile of sidewalk chalk, bubbles, cars, and blocks—plenty to keep them busy while I sat and watched. That started a bad habit, though. I began to use their outdoor playtimes as my excuse to be lazy, parked in a lawn chair so I could just do nothing.

I distinctly remember my son saying to me, "Please, Mommy, come and play," as he and his sister created works of art on the driveway with some sidewalk chalk. Then the following words floated through my head, *I've become a Sideline Mom*—one of those moms who sits and watches rather than participates.

God placed on my heart that day the importance of playing with my children, not just watching them play. If they were coloring, I was coloring. If they were singing into a hairbrush, you got it, watch out *American Idol*! I was either participating with them or very engaged with them while they were playing. It was an attitude of the heart, and my heart was now choosing to love through involvement.

Since that day, I have made a concerted effort to be a Fun Mom, not a Sideline Mom, and do things with my children more often than not. Neighbors used to think I was a bit crazy, as my front and side yard became a playland with toys strewn about, with me out there in the thick of it, blowing bubbles and creating works of art alongside my kids. But as my children have gotten older, they still ask me to "play" with them. Creating that habit and sticking with it is now allowing me the privilege of having teens who want to do things with their mom. That's an amazing gift in itself.

I know many of you may suffer from debilitating diseases that keep you from doing very active things with your children. Please understand that it's the *attitude* of the heart I'm talking about here. Children know when they're being brushed off. The point is to engage with your kids, show them that you want to spend time connecting with them, even if your health prevents you from very physical activity. Every child needs a mom who will encourage, ooh and aah, and cheer him or her on!

God does find a way of getting our attention and setting us back on the right path. On that day in the yard watching my children play, God took one simple sentence that slid through my brain, *I've become a Sideline Mom*, and reminded me that He had called me to be a mother and had blessed me with motherhood. My children couldn't "arise and call [me] blessed" (Proverbs 31:28) or receive the promise from the Ten Commandments if I was being a martyr. And I certainly couldn't raise my children well and keep a happy home with such an Eeyore attitude!

God also took things one step further, because as I started praying for the desire to get back on track, I felt Him saying to me that I needed to stop praying for the desire to "defluff" my body, my attitude, and my spiritual life. Instead, I needed to start praying for the discipline to get it done! Ouch!

Moms, anything you ever want to do well, you must practice, practice, practice, do, do, do over and over until it becomes habit, necessary even. We're very good at teaching that principle to our children. We teach them new words, encourage them to practice their piano exercises, quiz them when they need to memorize spelling words, and so on.

Our desire to release ourselves from a mom trap must be combined with action. Here's a standard that you may have never noodled on: Did you know that you cannot wait to "feel like" making changes? You have to just do it, force yourself to make the changes, and then you'll feel like it. I know that sounds backward, but it's true! Nike figured this out long ago; one of the greatest marketing campaigns of all time was their "Just Do It" campaign.

Part of you just doing it may include relaying some of your needs to your husband or family and friends. I had a discussion with my husband, explaining that I realized I had to have some time each day to myself. I had to have room to spend time praying and listening to God. I also realized that for my physical and mental well-being, I needed to move my body. I combined both needs, and praying while walking became my solution.

Bill and I decided that at least five days a week, I would walk or hike, and he would help me keep that commitment by making sure that if I didn't have the opportunity for this alone time before he got home from work, I would do it sometime after he got home. Sometimes the kids would be with me on a bike and/or a Big Wheel, so it wasn't always completely alone time, but it worked. At times it was while the kids were at school or preschool or on a playdate. Other times it was when my husband was home in the evenings. The thing was, it was a priority, and we made it happen.

For some of you, that may require getting a little help from a neighbor or a teenage babysitter, or looking for a great exercise DVD or a treadmill if you can't get help with the kids. Another option is doing an activity with your kids! Find the time of day that works best for you and your children, and make it a priority to move your body. When my walk-and-talk-time-with-God routine started, it definitely helped shut the Martyr Mom trap down.

Woe to Those Who Have to Live with Me

Tell me if any of the following sounds familiar to you: "Mom, where's my ChapStick?" "Honey, where are my work jeans?" "Hey, where did you put my backpack?"

Now, do these silent responses sound familiar: *Why am I the only person in this house who puts things back where they belong!? Are you serious? I wouldn't use your ChapStick no matter how cracked my lips are! Your pants don't fit me, and I'm scared of your backpack . . . it's filthy! Do they honestly think I have some sort of sixth sense that can determine where they put their stuff? Why does everyone ask me where stuff is?*

If you're a mom, I have a sneaking suspicion these scenarios are familiar to you. Have you ever had one of those days when you were fed up with having to be the mom? It seems like we always have to be the one who keeps up with everything. Having to be "on" and at everyone's beck and call 24/7 can leave us reacting with less than a gracious attitude. (Well . . . it can leave me doing that.)

At times I find myself wanting to scream, "I don't know! Why are you asking *me*?" But I work hard to hold my tongue. I try not to react in anger. At least, not out loud. Okay, I admit it; I do boil on the inside and get a bit snarky, with a "How am I supposed to know?" or a "Don't ask me!" or a top-notch dig, "Why do I have to do everything around here?!"

I've even had this nasty habit of vilifying everyone else in my family, carrying around this overarching feeling that I was being picked on and everyone else was the problem. I would get all bowed up as I camped on the thought that I was the only one in the house who ever did anything, and that no one ever appreciated me, which, in reality, wasn't true. Not only was that kind of thinking not true; it wasn't helpful.

I started recognizing when I was sinking into that mind-set and then intentionally labeling it as "I'm being a Martyr Mom." Instead of wallowing in despair, I took control of my feelings. Whenever I started having impatient thoughts toward my family or feeling the need to point out my sacrifices and efforts, I would bite my tongue, redirect my thought life, and *choose* a positive attitude. I'm not saying it's always easy, but it's doable. And *you* can do this, Mom.

While it's your decision to choose a positive attitude, rest assured that you don't have to do this alone. Don't think that my own goodness caused me to evaluate my reactions toward my family. It was and is the still small voice of the Holy Spirit that keeps advising me not to become a sniveling whiner or a raving lunatic.

○   ○   ○

I met Jennifer and instantly liked her; we seemed drawn to each other, as if we were friends before we were friends! Her soft-spoken nature complements the gentleness that is evident in her clear blue eyes and her servant's heart. She has her hands more than full with two daughters, one of whom has severe autism, but that doesn't keep her fingers from flying across a keyboard to offer help and hope to other frazzled moms.

She uses her gift of writing in the blog world (*www.jennifer dyer.net*). Who knew she had fallen into the Martyr Mom trap? Well, everyone knew, because she vulnerably wrote a blog post about it. She was kind enough to allow me to share it with you:

Yesterday, Lauren and I were driving on our way to get Rachel from school. We were listening to some kid CD, and I remarked that one of the characters was stingy.

"What's stingy, Mommy?" Lauren asked.

I blinked a few times—afternoon is not my best time of the day. I searched for words a six-year-old would understand. "Um, stingy . . . That's when a person is grumbly grouchy." Not a great definition, but it was the best my brain would give me.

She remained quiet for a moment. "So, you're stingy then." It wasn't really a question.

Hmm. That didn't go well. Before I got upset, I decided we should explore this a bit further.

"Why would you call me stingy?"

I could see her shrug in the rear-view mirror.

"You know, you can be all grumbly grouchy and stuff." She gave me that nod little ones do when they are saying something very grown up.

Ah. "I think I told you the wrong definition. I'm not stingy, but you're right, I can be a grouch sometimes."

Before I could redefine stingy, she interrupted, "That's okay, Mommy. I can be a grouch, too."

"Oh?"

"Yeah," she said with that same nod. "You know, like when I'm tired. Daddy does it, too."

I sighed. I often forget how perceptive children are. They pick up on even the smallest change in our voices. I thought back to my own childhood. I was a sensitive kid, and one of the things I appreciated most about my parents was when they admitted their shortcomings and were humble about them, even when it meant apologizing to my sister and me.

I smiled at her in the mirror. "I'm sorry Mommy acts like a grouch sometimes. It's not right to do that, is it?"

Again with the nod. "No, Mommy, but everyone does it. I'm sorry I act like one, too."

"Does Jesus want us to act like that?" I asked.

She giggled and looked out the window. "No, but He doesn't stay mad when we do."

I couldn't help but grin. It was a great bonding moment for us. There's something refreshing about being so open with others, especially my daughter. It's also taken a lot of the pressure off me as a parent. She knows I'm not flawless, but by being transparent about my shortcomings I hope to point her to the One who is perfect.[1]

Sometimes, when we're tired of being tugged on, questioned, or constantly needed, we can forget that children are so adorable, so teachable, so fun! Think of all those sweet, special memories every parent cherishes—that *you* cherish.

Little Eyes Are Watching (Big Ones, Too)

When my daughter was about nine, I did something she didn't exactly agree with, and she glared at me. I mean the look on her face was lethal. I remember thinking, *Uh-oh, you're in big trouble, young lady! Just why would you think it's acceptable for you to look at me like that?* Then God revealed the answer: *Because she learned it from you.*

So maybe I don't have a problem with yelling at my children (most of the time), but I obviously have a problem glowering at my children, because I've had the "favor" returned. If you glare, she glares. If you raise your voice in anger, he raises his voice in anger. If you're having a bad day, they're having a bad day. Why does that happen?

Kay Arthur is one of the most well-respected Christian leaders of our time, and she lives her life to share truth with others. In a video interview I did with her, she said something to me (and the moms I reach out to through social media) that literally made me want to grab her and give her a big ol' bear hug. She said, "Mom is the thermostat of the home!"

In my years of speaking into moms' lives, I have constantly tried to make them realize that they are the "temperature gauge" of their home! To hear this godly, loving woman speak that very same truth right to me literally made me feel as though God was confirming one of the core messages I've carried with me for years. Mom, it is so true that those "little eyes" look to you to determine how they will engage with their world on any given day.

Yes, I confess my children pick up my bad habits by watching me, but they also pick up the good ones. One of my constant prayers has been, "God, please magnify what I do right and minimize what I do wrong." Especially when I am grumbly grouchy!

I do hope you'll realize that your attitude is *your* choice, not someone else's fault. It was more than difficult and humbling for me to admit to myself that I was choosing to be pitiful and that it was my own doing. Not my husband's fault, not my children's fault, not motherhood's fault, and certainly not God's fault—my fault. Hard for me to admit about myself, but it's true. I hope and pray you'll save yourself from this trap by recognizing it's coming before it even happens.

Of course, being able to admit you've fallen into the Martyr Mom trap is hard but necessary if you want to replace Eeyore with more of a "T-I-double-guh-err?" type of attitude; you know, Pooh's friend Tigger . . . "bouncy, trouncy, flouncy, pouncy, fun, fun, fun, fun, fun!"[2]

But how in the world do we keep ourselves from grumbling, complaining, and being frustrated amid the demanding role of motherhood? When it comes to living an everyday momlife in the right way, our motto should be "attitude is everything." And when it comes to advice on attitude, the book of Proverbs is a great place to go:

> A happy heart makes the face cheerful,
>> but heartache crushes the spirit.
> The discerning heart seeks knowledge,
>> but the mouth of a fool feeds on folly.
> All the days of the oppressed are wretched,
>> but the cheerful heart has a continual feast.
>> (Proverbs 15:13-15)

Another way to change your heart attitude is by slipping away for a moment of quiet and a chance to regroup. I realize that at times slipping away isn't an option, so you might have to get creative.

When my children were younger, I had a signal that meant "Mom's had enough; she's on edge; you should give her some space." I would sit in a certain chair in the kitchen and mime that I was closing myself off in a closet. Until I opened the imaginary doors and stood up, they pretty much left me alone. I could see and hear everything, of course, but I pretended not to. My children used to just act as if I wasn't there. I would choose those precious moments to breathe deeply, lift up a prayer, and shake off the attitude that was destined to cause things to go south quickly.

One of the things my family has a tendency to tease me about is my habit of bursting out in song and/or dance for no apparent reason. Well, there is a reason. Each of those habits causes me to be joyful and lighthearted. It's rather hard to have a bad attitude and feel sorry for myself when I'm dancing in the kitchen, singing, "I got a couple dents in my fender, got a couple rips in my jeans!"[3] (Thank you so very much, Francesca Battistelli!)

Yes, music calms the savage beast! So find something that lightens your load and lifts your spirits, and use it daily, hourly, constantly—whatever it takes to keep you up. Draw, create, write, play your favorite music, dance and sing like a crazy woman—kids *like* crazy! Mom, like it or not, you and I set the thermostat for our homes. So be intentional in setting it to the right temperature.

Here's how God used this newfound realization in my life: The whole "No one appreciates me" Martyr Mom syndrome enabled me to see how others around me must feel. I try to use that knowledge to deepen my appreciation for those who serve me, whether at a restaurant, a bank, or a grocery store . . . or day after day in a classroom, teaching my child.

If you see someone who looks as if she's having a bad day, choose to be the person she interacts with that day who will encourage her and make her smile. Just recently at Walmart, the attendant at the counter for the "pay yourself" checkout lanes looked absolutely miserable. So I struck up a conversation with her and

mom truth ○○○○○○○○○○○○○○○○○○○○○

My inability to find enthusiasm and joy in everyday momlife wasn't the fault of my circumstances; it was the condition of my heart. The daily attitude a mom transfers to those within her home is a choice. You must embrace each day as an opportunity to influence those whom God has entrusted to you within your home and community.

said a few encouraging words. Her whole countenance changed! The bank tellers at the drive-through literally perk up when they see me now, because they know I'm always going to have a positive word for them.

Everyone has bad days; everyone has jobs that become monotonous and boring, so make it your job to be that ray of sunshine in your community and your home! It may sound simplistic or contrived, but it's not. My desire to cheer others is because I'm so often the one who needs cheering.

Learning this "Don't be a martyr" way of thinking was a major turning point in my life, a personal declarative where I had to decide whether I was living my life for me or for God. A very telling scripture in the Bible speaks to this sort of attitude, and I think it's especially important for moms: "Whatever you do, work at it with all your heart, as working for the Lord, not for men" (Colossians 3:23).

Making the decision to change my attitude and live my life for God caused me to commit to the discipline of learning more about Him and how He expects me to live. I could see firsthand that living for Him and doing things His way made my life, the lives of my family, and the lives of those around me better. No more learning about God a little here, a little there, but "all in," so to speak.

If you've always longed to discover yourself, let me assure you, the real answers are found in the discovery of God and His will for your life. God is pursuing a closer relationship with you right now; that's why you're reading these words. I hope you'll take time each day to pray. Simply talk to God, tell Him your thoughts and feelings.

If you recognize that you're in the Martyr Mom trap, please don't give up. It took me awhile—a lot of discipline and a lot of heart change—but by hearing God's voice above my own, I learned who I was meant to be.

Martyr-Mom-Trap Quiz

Please read the following statements and rate yourself on a scale from one (strongly agree) to five (strongly disagree). Journal some thoughts about each statement. Then answer the corresponding questions or follow the instructions.

1. I don't want to have a "poor pitiful me" attitude. _____

   List examples when you've had this attitude. (It's okay; we've all been there!)

2. I am a Fun Mom. _____

   List three times within the past week when you had fun with your children.

3. I currently try to live a healthy lifestyle and make time for God. _____

List specific commitments you will make to "just do it" (not wait until you "feel" like doing it). How will you practice discipline in these areas?

4. I approach serving others with joy. _____

What can you do to help yourself have an attitude of service with a smile?

5. I live my life for God, not myself. _____

How will you make that more of a reality in your life?

Scoring Chart

  5–8 = You approach serving as a mom with joy and a good attitude.

  9–12 = You get frustrated at times by your mom duties and need to examine your heart.

 13–16 = You are trying to serve your family well but are beginning to have feelings of resentment and frustration.

 17–20 = You are dangerously close to being trapped; you need to change course.

 21–25 = You are in the Martyr Mom trap, and you are desperate for rescue.

Next Up . . .

Once you are able to identify and avoid the Martyr Mom trap, I suggest you keep a close watch for the next logical trap that could come your way: the Busy Mom trap. With your newfound desire to serve with a happy heart, life can become all about getting lots done. That's a good thing, right? Let's explore that thought together!

CHAPTER 5

Busy Mom Trap

Supermom to the rescue!

My personality is generally that of a go-to girl. I can get it done and move from one thing to the next in a flurry. That's part of why I am a jack-of-all-trades! Yet I've noticed that I can get overwhelmed with all that has to be done and become a whirlwind of activity but not much fun to be around. A mom who's constantly busy, busy, busy. The Busy Mom trap catches those of us who figure that if we can get it all done and just stay busy enough, we'll be good moms. We say yes to most anything that's asked of us, because we'll be deemed successful moms and good moms if we're seen doing everything everywhere for everyone.

If you suspect that you've slipped into the Busy Mom trap, let me assure you that you are not alone. Allow me to pose two questions: What do you spend your time doing? And why do you spend your time doing it?

Whip out your to-do list, Momchick, and take a gander. We all got 'em; it's probably stuffed down in your purse or programmed into your phone! You have the "whats" written on the list. Is it voluminous and ominous? Mine generally is. Now, take a shot at scribbling down the "whys" next to the "whats."

What Am I Doing?

My to-do list is frequently my nemesis. I can be having a perfectly good day being a heroic mom of epic proportions; then I take one look at my to-do list (that seems to multiply tasks like bunny rabbits breed), and suddenly my shoulders slump and my hero's cape flutters downward in defeat. So much to do . . . so little time.

Then slowly and sneakily the perceived solution bubbles up from my exhausted brain, and I reason with myself that I simply must do more at a more rapid pace—squeeze it all in! That solution seems harmless enough, but actually, it's an endless cycle of never-ending duties and attempts at validation through task completion. Where's the joy in that?

An overwhelming to-do list causes a mom to be more focused on tasks rather than relationships. You think, *Sure I want to be a Fun Mom, but I have a laundry list of things to accomplish today. There are dust bunnies gathering in the corner, I haven't blogged in weeks, and I have to make cookies for the upcoming teacher luncheon.* Sound familiar?

Those things are important because they are how we live out serving our families and our communities. I'm not saying we should cast aside our responsibilities in order to play with our children. I *am* saying we need to establish priorities and find balance so that we can accomplish both.

And while we're talking about priorities and balance, let's tackle the whole "feeling guilty" thing, which is something all of us moms have experienced at one time or another. Just the other day a mom shared with me that she feels guilty when she's away from home working at her part-time job, and she also feels guilty when she's at home and not working.

My advice to her, you, and myself is this: Make sure your children know, I mean *really* know, that they matter more to you than the tasks you have to complete. Make it known to whomever you are working for, or volunteering for, that your children matter more than the task. When you're with your children, be fully with them.

I have a friend who speaks all over the country, and she tells anyone who invites her that she can only come if she is allowed to bring one of her children or her husband with her. That's some wise mommying right there! God knows your heart, Mom, and your children will feel your intentionality. Push that guilt away.

To be honest, I have gotten some grief from others over the fact that my husband and I travel several days a year for various engagements; however, I did the math. There are 365 days in a year. If I am away for 20 of those days, that actually allows my children 20 days of "doing life" with other godly families who they stay with when Bill and I are both traveling.

I've seen God use the time my kids spend with other families to reinforce what Bill and I are teaching them in our own home. It's amazing how God has used other moms to confirm many of the things I am trying to teach my children.

To Be or Not to Be

Are you a "be-er" or a doer?

My family and I took a trip to Rwanda in the summer of 2009. I learned an amazing truth while over in the land of a thousand hills: Always travel with Pepto-Bismol. No, wait . . . That's not the amazing truth! But I'm just sayin', take the pink with you if you ever travel there.

The people of Rwanda are known for surviving with little and doing without. Rwandans live simple lives; however, they stay busy because life is hard there. Though they spend their days surviving— carrying water buckets on their heads for miles and preparing their one family meal of the day—they don't spend their entire day *doing*. They know the importance of *being* and building relationships.

While we were there, we met with the Archbishop of the Anglican church and his entire council of bishops who come together once a year to discuss how they can best help and serve their people. After meeting for nearly an hour and sharing our desire to come alongside them to help strengthen families, they insisted we stop our meeting and have tea. It was time to stop the "meeting talk" and have "relationship talk" to get to know one another personally. They interrupted the doing to "be" with their guests.

My husband, our two teens, and I went on this trip to Rwanda, and the biggest impression it made on us was that we needed to reserve more time to be and less time to do, a concept that seems foreign in our culture. You've heard the phrase "Work hard and play hard," I'm sure. Unfortunately, here in America too many of us seem to have whipped out a pair of sharp, unforgiving scissors and snipped off the last three words of that phrase.

Think about it, Mom. Have you been sucked into the Busy Mom trap because you feel that to be a good mom, you must constantly be doing? Moms in this trap have a tendency to miss out on the special moments, the quiet moments, the silly and the fun moments throughout the day because stopping to enjoy such things would be considered a waste of time. They're so anxious to check off that next box on their to-do list that the joy of such moments is lost on them.

The Bible tells us the story of Mary and Martha. You see, Mary was a "be-er" and Martha was a doer. As a result, Martha missed out on sitting at the feet of Jesus and learning from Him, because she was just too busy to stop . . . even for Him.

As [Jesus and his disciples] continued their travel, Jesus entered a village. A woman by the name of Martha welcomed him and made him feel quite at home. She had a sister, Mary, who sat before the Master, hanging on every word he said. But Martha was pulled away by all she had to do in the kitchen. Later, she stepped in, interrupting them. "Master, don't you care that my sister has abandoned the kitchen to me? Tell her to lend me a hand."

The Master said, "Martha, dear Martha, you're fussing far too much and getting yourself worked up over nothing. One thing only is essential, and Mary has chosen it—it's the main course, and won't be taken from her." (Luke 10: 38-42, MSG)

Wow, Jesus wants us to realize that there are times we need to chill out on the details. When we're too worked up doing, we're not the only ones who suffer and miss out on the important things in life—our children miss out too.

I had a friend, who shall remain nameless, who was constantly on the go and doing, doing, doing. She was admired in her community, accomplished, dependable, and a go-getter. But she never had time for her child. It was painful to watch her child wither, and it seemed as though no amount of coaching, encouraging, and chastising from her fellow moms (who could see what was happening) could cause her to turn her heart toward home. The approval of others was more important to her than a relationship with her own child.

Watching this happen in her life gave me a wake-up call that a busy-is-better philosophy wouldn't help me be the best mom I could be. I shocked all those who knew me when I declared that for one year I was going to say no to extra commitments and concentrate solely on being a mom and a wife. Once I embraced this new lifestyle, it was actually fun to say no every time I was asked to do something! It kind of freaked out a few people. (Snicker, snicker. I confess . . . I liked it!)

After a year of saying no, I learned to pick and choose wisely what I would and would not do with my time. Here's an interesting word picture I like to use: I see my life as a shelf, and on the shelf is a group of glass jars. I am the proud caretaker of a jar for myself, my husband, each child, and all my activities. If ten jars are already on the shelf and I'm asked to do something . . . well, another jar won't fit. So I have to choose which jar I'm going to take off the shelf so that I can put that new jar up there.

This concept made me realize that each yes to something requires a no to something else. I have to prayerfully consider what is and what isn't worth my time and energy.

And speaking of those glass jars . . . Another thing to keep in mind is the truth that you are teaching your children how to use their time, too. You don't want to teach your children to be too busy for their own children someday. Remember, those children will be *your* adorable grandchildren. Since every grandparent I know says that having grandchildren is the best part of life, watch what you teach the future parent of your grandchild!

There's a saying I've carried with me for years: "If the Devil can't make you bad, he'll make you busy." Sweet, well-intentioned Busy Moms out there, please allow me to say from one Busy Mom to another, it really is okay to say no. Really. Anyone can be busy, but only you can be a mom to the children God has blessed you with. I double-dog dare you to embrace a year of no's and see what you learn.

I encourage you to prioritize your life. You can't do your best at anything if you're doing too much of everything. Count your jars and recognize that if you try to shove another jar onto your shelf, a very precious jar may just fall off and shatter.

Answer the following questions:

1. Do you know the why behind what you have to do? Get out your to-do list, and beside each to-do, answer the question Why?

2. How much time do you spend each day doing versus being? (Sleep doesn't count toward either.)
3. During your being time, what do you do?
4. How can you live out being with each of your family members? Formulate a new "to be" list (instead of your to-do list), and jot down a few ideas of how you can spend time with each family member. Carry that list around with you!

Sometimes being happens accidentally, but you usually have to look for opportunities. I learned long ago that if my child wanders into the room when I'm in task mode, I can stop what I'm doing and spend some intentional time to be with him. When he's ready to move on, he'll go off and do his own thing again, and then I can finish up my task. That way, the task is left waiting, not my child.

In case you think I have this all figured out, I was having a conversation with my daughter a few months ago, and she was telling me something about her day. I was sort of listening—my laptop was open, and I'm guessing my eyes were glazed over and I was nodding, uttering "yeah" every now and then. Suddenly I heard her say something like, "And then the elephant stampeded right through the restaurant, and tables went flying everywhere." I jerked my head up and said, "What? Where were you?" She grinned and shook her head. She had caught me.

Mom, your children need you, all of you—your ears, your smile, your eyes! Take time to connect with them, eyeball to eyeball, heart to heart! We all need to listen to our children, pay attention to them, be with them, and hang out with them. Be the mom!

I have a friend who, at times, has felt slighted by me because I seem to spend so much time at home with my children. She once asked me what I always do with my children. Well, interestingly, we don't always do something. Sometimes we just "be." Sure, we do things because I like adventure and so do they. But everyday togetherness is an adventure too, because my children know I'm interested in them and enjoy being around them. And, to be honest, my children have helped loosen me from the Busy Mom trap by teaching me how to chill quite well.

When my son was a little boy, every Tuesday and Thursday when I picked him up from preschool we would come home, eat lunch, and then curl up on the couch together and watch *Tom and Jerry*. It was part of our regular weekly routine, our special time to do absolutely nothing together except cuddle and giggle.

Well, that little boy is now a teenager, over six feet tall, 185 pounds, and about as much an outdoorsman as a teen could be. Recently when he was home sick from school, he was sprawled out on my couch, his large frame spilling off the edge, and he yelled at me, "Mom, come here! *Tom and Jerry* is on!"

My to-do list was dripping off of the page; I was sitting at my computer trying to get something done. But I stopped, walked away, plopped down on the chair, and watched *Tom and Jerry* with my "little" boy. We were laughing here and there, glancing at each other and smiling. At one point he said, "Hey, Mom, you like this one. It's the one with the little seal in it!"

Think with me a moment of all the things that could have been occupying my teenage son's time while he was home sick from school. But there sat my fifteen-year-old, watching *Tom and Jerry* and wanting me to watch it with him. Trust me, taking the time to be with your children is a very important investment of your time.

Being = Relationship

Does it work? Does being instead of doing matter? I sure think so.

One of my dearest friends, Dana, is a single mom, and even

with a demanding full-time job, she is always looking for ways to be with her son and do the things he likes to do. He has an eBay business she helps him with, and he collects coins and knives, both of which she knows more about than she ever cared to. I can't tell you how many movies she's watched with her son that she wouldn't normally choose to watch. In fact, *my* son counts on her to call and offer to bring him along on these epic movie-watching adventures with her son.

Last summer, Dana took her son and mine on a one-week vacation to two of the greatest amusements parks in the country. It wasn't a vacation she would have chosen for herself, and it required a lot of driving, but she did it and created amazing memories along the way. She also earned some serious cool-mom points for that one!

We all have responsibilities we must attend to, but it's so important to carve out special times to do fun things with our kids—vacations, day trips to parks, or even pajama days where we hang out at home and do simple fun things they want to do! Let your kids choose how you'll spend that fun day!

Kids love traditions. If you and your husband work outside the home, consider making Friday nights "Family Night." Grab a pizza and a board game, a video game, or a movie, and have the whole family chill together after a long hard week. Or make Sunday nights "Story Night," and read, put on plays, or tell stories from your childhood or your kids' early years. Our family makes up stories together to spark our creativity and imagination.

Yes, there are things that have to get done around the house, but spread the workload out among the family. This allows extra time to enjoy your children; they are amazing, after all. And remember what we learned from the Me Mom trap: It doesn't have to be done your way; it just has to be done.

Allow me to say a word about the newest Busy Mom trap

that's a major time stealer, and a sneaky one at that. I mean suddenly an hour is gone, and I can't figure out where it went! Moms, I, too, very much enjoy social media, and I've had to be very intentional about not allowing it to take my attention away from my family. Here's one way to do this: Tell your family members to hold you accountable regarding time online. I've heard each of my family members say to me, "Hey, you've been on that computer too long! Remember, you said . . ." When I hear that, I listen and step away.

Family comes first, and social media needs to be put on hold, not your spouse and children! Your most important fans and followers are those you live with, and they need to see your eyes, not the top of your head! (You can tweet me on that!)

Why Am I "Doing"?

When you meet up with another mom, have you ever gone back and forth through the whole "Hello, how are you? What's going on with you? I am *so* busy; I just can't seem to stop! I have so much to do!" The mom who sounds the busiest wins! I fear the Busy Mom trap causes us to thrive off one-upping others and receiving the admiration from people around us who think we're successful in life because we're so busy.

As I search my own behavior patterns, I catch myself thriving off the accolades of others: "Wow, look at you! You can do it all. You are the busiest woman I know!" Or I get far too excited over a list marred by check marks—taking that pen or cursor and checking off yet another item on my ever-increasing to-do list. Proof, right there in black and white, that I'm a successful, involved mom.

One of the really alarming habits of a Busy Mom is her tendency to teach her busy habits to her children by vicariously living her own life through them and their accomplishments. Busy Mom pushes and pushes her children to be active at school, in athletics, in social activities, in an all-out "Whose kid is the best?" and "My kid can do more than your kid" competition to the nth degree!

That "My kid can do more than your kid" competition can get out of control quickly. I have sat on the bleachers during such a competition, and when other moms whip out the "My child is involved with . . ." laundry list, I politely listen and make the choice not to compete. It's too exhausting. And it's loads more fun just letting the other mom win and watching her confusion when I don't whip out my own brag list. My advice to you, Mom, is don't play the game.

This trap can sneak up on you because human nature lures you to be competitive. You need to remember that sometimes, even worthwhile activities can rob you from precious time with your family. You could be dragged into the trap before you even know it's there. That's why it's called a trap! So be on the lookout, Mom!

Mom Thoughts vs. Woman Thoughts

Recently a friend of mine told me she didn't know how to be happy. That shocking statement caused me to pause and contemplate the reasoning behind it. It has also caused me to think a lot about you, me, us—moms and the issue of happiness.

Before motherhood, most of us had ample opportunity to pursue what "filled our tank" or made us happy. The world and our futures lay before us. Every day we made choices that were largely based on our own personal needs. Happy was readily available because we pretty much could acquire what we wanted or needed on a daily basis. But once we become moms, something changes inside, and suddenly our own needs seem secondary, and the well-being of our children takes precedence—and absolutely, this is as it should be. (We'll talk about this a little more in the They Say Mom chapter.)

Once I became a mom, I changed the way I made decisions. Decisions that were once made by Tracey the woman started being made by Tracey the mom. For many of us, this "dying to self" can alter our "happy." Allow me to give you a few examples. I wanted to take a class, but I chose to take one that was offered at night, when Bill could be home with the kids. I wanted to start a business, so I chose selling children's clothing out of my home. I wanted to get into photography, but because it was very time consuming and expensive, I had to pass on that one!

When I wanted to be a volunteer at a local women's clinic, I waited until my youngest started preschool so I could volunteer while the kids were at school. Each decision had to consider what Tracey the woman wanted but was ultimately determined by what Tracey the mom believed was best for the family.

To give your mom thoughts priority above your woman thoughts, will you have to make personal sacrifices? Yes. Will it be less than the perfect scenario? Yes. Will you always get your way? No. Is that a bad thing? No.

Our happiness should not be based on our circumstances; rather than seeking "happy" we need to seek contentment. Philippians 4:11 instructs us "to be content whatever the circumstances." I think sometimes the result of the "mom thoughts" versus "woman thoughts" decision-making process is that a mom can lose sight of what the woman in her enjoys. It's true that while in the thick of mothering, you may not be able to pursue those dreams as fully as you might like, but I want to encourage you not to lose sight of what makes you happy. Write down your dreams and what you want to accomplish in life. Find ways to still participate in what the woman in you wants, but not at the expense of silencing the mom in you.

Get out that list of what "fills your tank" and find opportunities to pull out those paint brushes, that bicycle, your camera, or your grandmother's recipe cards and carve out a time—maybe once a week or once a month—to allow your tank to be filled. Remember that even flowers are planted and grown in all seasons. And trust me on this, your mom decisions and the growth you experience as a result will place you on the road to finding and fulfilling the true God-inspired dreams of your woman heart.

In his book *Quitter*, Jon Acuff discusses with his readers the very real truth that the daily monotonous tasks we want to flee from and quit are the very things preparing us for our dreams of the future. He makes a thought-provoking case for this concept with his "platform and the prison" principle that he describes as follows: "If you're patient and deliberate, your day job [in our case motherhood] can become a wonderful platform from which you can launch your dream job. If you demonize your day job though and rail against it, it becomes a prison you'll try to escape from. And prison breaks rarely go well for anyone."[1]

Mr. Acuff brilliantly outlines the importance of doing the mundane and daily tasks in preparation for the grand future dreams God has placed in every person's heart, and he skillfully points out that there are truly no shortcuts to steadfastness. Time, experience, and reflection lead to wisdom that cannot be rushed, Mom, so enjoy the journey. Realize that slow and steady wins the race to achieved dreams. Appreciate the certainty that God is growing you through the mom process so that you can be the woman He has designed you to be.

Many Hands Make Less Busy Moms

Here's an interesting thought: What if your doing stuff is keeping someone else from growing by serving? I used to have this tendency to think that just because I *could* do something, I *should* be the one to do it. I was always quick to do whatever was asked of me, regardless of the cost to my family time. What's the harm in that? A dear, sweet friend who was older and wiser pointed out to me that as long as I took the lead and tried to do it all, I was actually keeping someone else from stepping forward to pitch in and use *her* gifts.

Let that sink in a bit there, Mrs. Busy Mom. Do you leap at the chance to do, and is part of your motivation to receive public recognition or peer acceptance? In the process, are you taking on so much that you're keeping others from serving? I have been in enough volunteer meetings to know that if you're still and quiet long enough, someone else will raise her hand. Remember the old adage "Many hands make less Busy Moms"? (Okay, so the old adage is "Many hands make light work," but now we have a new twenty-first-century adage!)

My suggestion that you not volunteer so much doesn't mean you cease to serve. God wants you to use your gifts and talents. I am simply suggesting you learn to serve for all the right reasons without

mom truth °°°°°°°°°°°°°°°°°°°°°°°

I am the only mom my children have, and though I can multitask, I need to be mindful of what I spend my time doing and why I am doing it. Making time to be with your children and care for your family, while accomplishing goals, can be done with careful, thoughtful decision-making. Being a busy mom is not the goal; instead, being a relational and content mom is what you should strive for.

sacrificing your family relationships in the process. Our main priority in decision-making needs to be what is best for our own health and the well-being of our family.

I suggest you make it a point to measure the value of your time against your to-do list and those requests others make of you. I have a friend who makes it a practice to never immediately answer when someone asks her to do something. Her standard answer is "I need to think and pray about that and get back to you. When do you need to know?" After analyzing her and her family's commitments and schedules, she comes back with an answer, such as, "Yes, I can give you _____ hours a month to do that," or "No, that isn't what's best for my family right now." That's a wise practice for every mom to follow.

Many moms who are struggling in their relationships with their teens have approached me, heartbroken and seeking advice. They cannot figure out why they don't connect with their teenagers. It's my belief that the Busy Mom trap robs children of relationships with their moms.

Determine how you can shorten your to-do list in order to spend time with your children now, so that down the line when they are teens, you'll have earned the relational equity to be able to speak into their lives. If not, they'll get their cues and advice from peers. The Bible has something very interesting to say about your children's peers, especially the ones you have concerns about: "Do not be misled: Bad company corrupts good character" (1 Corinthians 15:33). I'm not saying that all teens are bad or that they will have a negative influence on your child, but simply that teens lack full-circle wisdom, and during the teenage years parental advice is the wisest.

I hope you're now convinced that the title "Busy Mom" isn't a badge of honor but a red flag indicating that you need to make some adjustments in the way you spend your time. From now on, when a mom friend asks, "So, how are you doing?" instead of replying, "I'm so busy!" consider sharing the last few fun things you've done with your kids. You might just influence her to do the same!

Busy-Mom-Trap Quiz

Please read the following statements and rate yourself on a scale from one (strongly agree) to five (strongly disagree). Then answer the corresponding questions or follow the instructions.

1. I am not a Busy Mom; I make lots of time for my children. _____

   List two special times you shared with your children this week.

2. My to-do list isn't a higher priority in my life than spending time with my children. _____

   Give an example of when you chose being with your children over an item on your to-do list.

3. I will consider saying no to extra commitments for a year. _____

Make a list of the current number of jars sitting on your shelf.

4. I give my children my full attention, with eyes and ears, and spend time just hanging out with them. _____

Record the last time you stopped and just hung out with your children.

5. I spend more time with my children than I do with media (TV, computer, phone). _____

How much time per day do you spend doing media-related things? Will you ask your family to hold you accountable for the time you spend doing those things rather than being with them? Why or why not?

Scoring Chart

5–8 = You are not a Busy Mom. You have made it a priority to spend time with your children.

9–12 = You make time for your children but also keep an eye on your to-do list.

13–16 = You are trying to live a balanced momlife, but your calendar is rather full.

17–20 = You spend a lot of time in task mode and are headed for the Busy Mom trap.

21–25 = You are in the Busy Mom trap and need to accept the double-dog dare of saying no for a year—lest a valuable jar slip off your shelf and shatter.

Next Up . . .

There is a hidden danger lurking among all those Busy Moms out there; we can get so wrapped up in all our busyness that we start to look around to see what all those other women are up to. We begin to think, *Maybe I need to remain a Busy Mom to keep up with the neighbor next door. Is she a better mom than I am? Am I measuring up?* We've all fallen into the Mirror Mom trap at one point or another. The good news is that there is a way to escape. Keep reading!

CHAPTER 6

Mirror Mom Trap

Who's the fairest?

A few years back, a trap that is familiar to all women snuck up on me and held me in its firm, strangling grip, leaving me wilted. At first it seemed like a harmless little game of comparison, especially if I was winning, but it actually led to discontentment. Maybe you've been there too. If you see your reflection shimmering in the Mirror Mom trap, trust me, unless you take the necessary steps to escape it, in the long run you'll shatter in its shallowness.

My great-great-grandmother had it way easier than I do. When she went out back in the garden to get the vegetables for the evening meal, she didn't face what I face every time I stand in line at the grocery store. I see magazine after magazine with covers displaying airbrushed, beautiful, powerful women with exciting, glamorous lives.

Great-great-grandmother came back from the garden feeling pretty spunky and good about herself as she tucked a daisy behind her ear and whistled a happy tune. I, on the other hand, on the way back from my garden (Walmart) have, at times, felt unbrushed, ordinary, and weak, with a mundane, boring life. One particular day, these feelings led me to tuck my ponytail behind my disheveled head and schlep into the house, feeling like I didn't measure up.

It wasn't just the magazine covers I didn't measure up to. I didn't measure up to the neighbors either. Check her out: great looks, great clothes, a better car, a better house, lots of friends, a tight social circle. Stuck in the Mirror Mom trap, as I looked around me, it appeared that everyone else was doing so much better and having so much more fun than I was. As I checked out the landscape of my next-door neighbor, I ultimately felt inadequate in comparison, like I didn't measure up and was missing out on something.

Appearing Daily

One of our family moves took us to a town in Texas, and we unknowingly bought a home in a neighborhood that had a reputation. Soon after we arrived and I started meeting people, I began noticing a pattern when they asked me where I lived. I would tell them the name of the street, and invariably they asked the question, "Which side of Harrison do you live on?" When I gave my answer, I was given a smile and a little nod of approval. Seems we bought ourselves a home right smack-dab in the middle of the "preferred" neighborhood.

Our new address set me up to fall straight into the Mirror Mom trap. Let's just say I was a Kentucky Avenue simple girl who found myself next to row after row of Park Place beauties. (Think Monopoly board, ladies.) Not long after we got settled in our home, I was invited to a neighbor's home party that showcased a designer clothing line. We could browse and buy right there in her home. I thought it was a kind gesture to invite the new girl on the block, and I figured it would be an opportunity to meet the neighbors. I like clothes, so what could be the harm?

I walked through that house, and it was all I could do not to turn tail and run with the intention of becoming a permanent hermit. The women there were perfectly coiffed and dressed in the kind of clothes I had never had on my simple little body. (Even when I worked on the island of Palm Beach among the rich and famous, I still shopped at discount-type stores.) I searched and searched for a piece of clothing I could rationalize buying, so as not to be a shabby neighbor.

The least expensive item I could find was a bright-orange tank top that was more than two hundred dollars. I kept stalling for time and trying to be pleasant, but I felt like every other woman in the house was looking at me as if I were Anne Hathaway's character in *The Devil Wears Prada*—clueless about style and fashion. I decided there was only one way out: I'd have to tell my neighbor the cold hard truth. I thanked her for inviting me, told her I thought the clothes were beautiful, and explained to her that I preferred to spend my money on items for my family and home rather than myself.

I politely and quickly scooted out the door, with my head held as high as I could muster, wondering what a Southern lady should do at a time like this. I tried to laugh it off, but there was no escaping it. I had tripped into the "How do I measure up to other women?" Mirror Mom trap.

I began to drag around this ugly trap, this hurtful feeling that because of my family-first lifestyle and my ordinariness, I was missing out on something. This got me wondering if the grass was greener on my neighbor's side of the fence, and I felt the temptation to jump the fence and start nibbling. I wrestled with the fact that the women around me seemed to have very exciting lives, and mine was unexciting. They always seemed to be going to such interesting places and doing such interesting things.

At times, being a mom and making our families a priority can begin to wear on the most determined of us, which can cause us to lose sight of the advantages of working to build strong, healthy relationships in our homes. We might then start to explore ways to measure up to those around us.

A Barna poll asked the question, "What constitutes the ideal life to you?"[1] The following top six answers might surprise you:

- Having good physical health   85%
- Living with a high degree of integrity   85%
- Having one marriage partner for life   80%
- Having a clear purpose for living   77%
- Having a close relationship with God   75%
- Having close personal friends   75%

Of these six sought-after life goals of Americans, you have within your grasp the ability to attain each one. In fact, I would bet that if you made building up the lives within your home a priority, you'd soon achieve the "ideal" life reflected in this poll.

The Mirror Mom trap warps the true image of the priorities of your life, causing you to want to chase the wrong ideals. Ideals such as a bigger or nicer home, a better wardrobe, a brand-new car, the latest technology gadget—you get the idea; superficial ideals rather than meaningful ideals. Instant gratification instead of sticking to long-term family goals.

One of the best examples I've seen of sticking to family goals is Crystal Paine, aka Money Saving Mom. (You can visit her at *www.MoneySavingMom.com*.) Crystal and her husband formulated a plan for their family goals of staying out of debt, finding a way to do life while keeping home a priority, and giving away lots of money to worthy causes.

They have worked hard and made sacrifices daily to stick to their long-term goals. They've refused to allow daily frustrations and circumstances to steer them off course, and they are living a full, happy life without trying to keep up with the Joneses. I don't tell you this so you'll compare yourself to the Paine family; just be encouraged that staying true to your own plan is possible!

The truth here? You must look at *your* life! Not listen to "If you compare yourself to *her*, how are you measuring up?" We all have this tendency to think Mrs. Jones's life is better than ours, and as a result, we spend valuable time worrying about our "less than-ness." What if I told you, "Where you have envy and selfish ambition, there you find disorder and every evil practice"? Well, actually, I didn't tell you that, James the brother of Jesus tells us that in James 3:16.

Have you, like me, ever looked in the mirror and berated yourself for your failures as a mom and a wife? That sounds like disorder and an evil practice to me, because it is destructive to you and ultimately to your children! Recently while spending the weekend with my daughter at college, I noticed this sign posted on the dorm floor bathroom mirror: "Comparison is the thief of joy!" Whoever placed that sign there is a wise young lady. Maybe we all need to post that on our bathroom mirrors!

In spite of the dialogue you and I may have with ourselves as we're peering at our reflections, allow me to share some truth with you, little lady. Here are the ABCs of what I know to be true because of who God is:

You are **ADORED** and **APPRECIATED**—God enjoys the crinkle in your nose when you smile, and He knows how magnificently special you are. He made you. He sees you when you feel overwhelmed and underequipped. He wants you to cast your cares on Him (1 Peter 5:7) and let loose big ol' belly laughs daily to sustain your joy.

You are **BEAUTIFUL** and **BRAVE**—God sees your unique beauty gloriously displayed in the gentleness of your eyes and the curve of your smile. Your inner splendor is evidenced by your selfless actions intuitively lavished on your family. He recognizes that being a mom is hard work, but you do it anyway, and He celebrates your triumph with an enchanting sunset to draw your overflowing heart toward Him.

You are **CAPTIVATING** and **CELEBRATED**—God draws near when you share the quiet heartfelt moments of love with the children He has entrusted to you. He knows you are the perfect mom for your children. He wants you right where He has you, and He wants to calm your soul with the quiet assurance that all is well.

Now, go look in the mirror and see yourself the way God sees you. I'm headed there myself.

○   ○   ○

With the challenges of motherhood, I have had personal struggles going from professional woman to exhausted mom to volunteer-entrepreneur mom. Sometimes this process has left me looking out into the world and then turning to the mirror to establish my value as a person. But I've learned not to allow comparisons with others, or others' opinions of me, to dictate who I am. Think about it. Why do we allow the opinions of others to be a part of our reflection instead of embracing the opinion of the One who designed us?

I am reminded of the now famous line in Kathryn Stockett's book and movie *The Help*, "You is kind. You is smart. You is important."[2] These three simple statements were spoken to the much-ignored daughter of a socialite, and the woman who lovingly raised her asked her to repeat them daily. This small-town, descriptive novel depicts what happens when women begin to place their value on status rather than on their God-given mandate to be the mom.

Remember the ABCs of mom truth and repeat them daily in the mirror. You are adored and appreciated. You are beautiful and brave. You are captivating and celebrated.

Who Is the Fairest?

All women struggle with finding their place among other women, whether in the executive boardroom or on the neighborhood playground. You can approach the Mirror Mom trap with an "I will be better than her at all costs" attitude, which could launch you back into one of the previously discussed traps. Or you can embrace the fact that you don't need to compare yourself to others. You just need to be comfortable with who you are and live your life as God has called you to, no matter what those around you are doing.

As more and more moms spend time on the Internet, involved with social media, the risk of falling into the Mirror Mom trap is even greater. As you move from site to site, you may find yourself measuring your worth and value by comparing your life to someone else's. By comparing how many followers she has, how many comments she's collected, and who retweets all of her tweets. And as you're trying to find your voice on the Internet, you will no doubt find someone who writes more eloquently, has more funny stories to tell, and posts more amazing photos on her site! We need not look for how we measure up against each other, but for how we can support one another as women and as moms. Share, don't compare.

Why is it that women need each other so much but tend to compare and judge themselves so harshly when they meet up? Remember the story of *Snow White*? Just what was the queen looking for when she asked the question, "Who is the fairest one of all?" She wanted the mirror to tell her how she measured up. Comparison is a dangerous vice. Rather than comparing ourselves to each other, we should enhance each other. A rose is beautiful, and so is a daisy, a dandelion, or a thistle. (Be honest, you know some thistles, and they definitely keep it interesting.)

From the time I was a little girl, I can remember my mother telling me to stand in front of the mirror and say positive things about myself. She understood that how others treated me could skew my view of myself, and she wanted me to like who I was. She believed in me, and she wanted me to believe in myself and my own self-worth. (Thanks, Mom!)

My grandmother taught me to be confident in who I am in Christ. She told me that my job in this world is to "love Jesus and love others as Jesus loves them. Because love is what is most important." Remember I told you my grandmother read the Bible all the time? That's where she learned Matthew 22:37-39: " 'Love the Lord your God with all your heart and with all your soul and with all your mind.' This is the first and greatest commandment. And the second is like it: 'Love your neighbor as yourself.' "

If your mind-set is to compare yourself to others and search the mirror for your own imperfections (or your own fabulousness), then you'll be stuck in a never-ending cycle of discontentment. There will always be someone prettier or more accomplished than you, and conversely, you'll always find someone you outshine. Either way, hurt feelings or haughtiness, yours or hers, will swell up, and your relationship will be thwarted.

Other Reflections

Interestingly, sometimes the epic void between two women can be obvious, but only to the one feeling shunned. Often, the offender isn't even aware of the issue. You've been there. It's that feeling of *Why doesn't she like me?* The not being invited, the avoided conversations, the knowledge that you could be her friend if she'd let you, the standing and staring into the mirror, thinking, *What's wrong with me?*

Are emotions welling up in you right now as you call up those feelings? Here's something you may never have considered: More than likely, you've caused those same welled-up feelings in someone else. That's the result of the Mirror Mom trap; there is a two-sided reflection, and sometimes we don't even know it!

To combat hurt feelings and not go down the road of comparison, we all need to view others charitably. Put another way: Always assume the best. In most cases, no one is out to hurt you, and you needn't wear your heart on your sleeve. On those occasions when someone is purposely unkind, you must learn to walk away. The Bible tells us to turn the other cheek (Matthew 5:39) and to forgive those who offend us (Colossians 3:12 14). It's not easy, I know. I've been there too.

In those situations, turning the other cheek might look like praying for the offender and forgiving, letting go of the hurt. But let me also practically advise you not to be held hostage by someone who is hurtful toward you. Sadly, she's probably behaving that way because she feels threatened by you. As a result, she'll either tear you down to make herself feel better or build herself up to make you feel worse.

In that way, she may feel as though you are equal to or less than her, and so she may feel less threatened. Sometimes you need to acquire the ability to ignore others and block out their hurtful words and actions as a means of self-preservation. In Matthew 10:14, even Jesus told His disciples to shake the dust from their feet and move on if they weren't welcomed in a town. Simply walk away and accept that a friendship with that person isn't going to happen, and that's okay. You don't have to allow it to make you feel downcast or bad about yourself. One of my favorite sayings is "You cannot steal my joy!" I say it aloud all the time.

When you feel hurt by another woman and your joy gets zapped, more often than not, she will be completely unaware of her offense toward you. Why? Because most people are very busy with their own lives, and they certainly aren't making decisions for themselves or their families based on your needs.

The next time you feel offended by someone, first ask yourself if you may be at fault because you're too easily offended. At least consider the possibility. Remember, just as you need grace from others, you need to extend grace to the women in your life. Simply said, don't dwell on it. Skip over it and give that person grace. I've learned that once this becomes a habit, life is sweeter. The inability to extend grace can lead to bitterness and allow misunderstandings to end friendships and affect your home life. When you retreat and isolate yourself, that's when the Mirror Mom trap can lead to despair, loneliness, and depression.

Rather than allowing the Mirror Mom trap to alienate you from other women, why not become a world changer and work with a group of women to do something amazing for others? My friend Barbara Rainey, cofounder of FamilyLife (*www.familylife. com*), teaches and encourages women to find something they're passionate about and utilize their time to be a world changer for God.

I know firsthand that one of the best ways to make meaningful friendships with women is to focus together on doing something for others, through volunteering and service projects. For example, several women in my neighborhood got together and started making meals for a sweet older couple who were experiencing health problems. Coming together to meet a common need fostered mutual admiration, not competition.

My friend Shannon (*www.myshannonigans.com*) gathers a group of moms together each year to serve others by having a "free" yard sale for families in need. The amazing thing is that after these families carefully make their selections, some come back hours later to donate items for future shoppers. These moms have created something helpful and life-giving to others. Rather than waste time staring in the mirror wondering who is fairer, they've learned that together they are a thing of beauty, through their service to others.

God desires us to be in relationship with Him and others, but He clearly advises us to be mindful of whom we spend time with and what we spend our time doing. Just as godly friendships can strengthen and uplift women, the reverse of that is also true: Toxic friendships are, quite frankly, a very powerful trap.

A few years ago I experienced real pain when I lost a friend through her own decision to shut me and the rest of her close friends out of her life. She simply walked away from her husband and sons and cut all ties with her church and her circle of friends. She became so focused on what "Mrs. Jones" was doing that she drifted far from God.

Several months prior to leaving her husband, she had begun spending time with a group of women who were influencing her in toxic ways, making her discontent and unhappy with her life. Through the whispers of these women, it appears she was pulled from her reality. The Mirror Mom trap led her to actually leave her family. My heart breaks when I remember the woman she once was, because she has moved so far from that.

I also regret that I didn't do more to question what was happening right before my eyes. When I noticed her pulling away from her family and our friendship, I should have intervened and spoken truth into her life, not given her space. I now know to speak up when I see a friend becoming more self-focused and less God-focused. There are women in my life who would do the same for me. I believe God places people in our path so that we can lift each other up and hold each other accountable.

I've learned the hard way that a missed opportunity for brave intervention can lead to disaster. This doesn't mean we should be looking for faults in our friends, but we need to be sensitive to God's promptings to come alongside in times of crisis and speak truth.

I encourage you to seek out friendships with women whose lives you respect and whose habits you want to rub off on you. Deep, abiding friendships can be one of the greatest joys in your life. As a rule of thumb, parents usually end up being friends with the parents of their children's friends, so be intentional about who your children spend time with, and pursue friendship with the whole family.

Start with an invitation for dessert and coffee as a get-to-know-you time; then follow up with a dinner invitation. Don't get discouraged if people don't initially invite you back; some just don't do hospitality well. That isn't necessarily an indicator of their lack of interest, just a lack of capacity. Remember, be quick to give grace to others.

Accountability and Relationship

I would also like to suggest something that you may be unfamiliar with or have never attempted to do but should: Get yourself an accountability partner. Every woman needs at least one friend who is in her corner, holding her accountable, offering support and encouragement, and sharing life with her.

Find someone you respect and admire. Perhaps she's further in her walk with God than you currently are, or maybe she's more experienced when it comes to parenting. Meet once a week, even if the meeting is over the phone or via the Internet because you're in a season of life when getting together isn't possible. If you don't know of such a person, find a church and ask about a mentorship program, or speak with a personal online mentor at *www.familylife. com/mentor.*

The most important thing women can do for each other is to be caring, listening friends. Strengthening each other through the truth found in God's Word, as well as prayer and fellowship, is also healing when we run into difficult situations. Proverbs 13:20 tells us, "He [she] who walks with the wise grows wise, but a companion of fools suffers harm." An accountability partner can help you find hope when your vision is too blurred to see it yourself. She'll remind you that God is working in your life even if you can't see Him. She'll help you trust what God says in His Word, scriptures such as John 11:40: "Then Jesus said, 'Did I not tell you that if you believed, you would see the glory of God?'"

My dear friend Marti struggled through two miscarriages and truly was losing hope of ever having a biological child. Through each loss and trial I loved her, prayed with her, and believed with her. When she became pregnant for the third time and was fearful and hurting, I was able to remind her of God's goodness and all that He had shown her in her past. We met together regularly, and on the days she was filled with anticipation, we celebrated together. But on the days she was filled with fear and what-ifs and began to lose hope, I wouldn't allow her to. She's now the very happy and blessed mother of Isabel Hope. God is good.

My friend Marilyn and I, although miles apart, hold each other up and give each other hope and clarity when the world seems to be fighting against us. There are times when I've been at the end of my rope, and I literally ache to speak with Marilyn because I know that she will absorb my words and offer wisdom and truth in love back to me. All the things I need to hear.

If you think it's just too hard to develop strong friendships, let me encourage you to make the decision to reach out and see what happens. God will provide. When we moved several years ago, I felt as though I was never going to find ongoing, meaningful relationships, but I didn't give up.

I had learned from past experience that different friendships have different purposes, and each is a gift that should be appreciated. I had to be patient and enjoy the acquaintances and friendships I was making while I waited for those women who really wanted to do life together to reveal themselves in returned phone calls and efforts to get together. I knew that while being grateful for each new friend, I needed to anticipate the abiding friendships that God would provide—and He did.

I also fulfilled a desire I'd had for years by inviting some ladies to come to my home once a month for a book-club meeting. Every time I'd thought of starting a book club in the past, I would chicken out or wonder what would happen if we all didn't get along, or if no one said yes to my invitation . . . The excuses were plentiful. But a few years ago, I bit the bullet, went for it, and invited three ladies to come to my home for lunch, mentioning that I was interested in starting a book club.

Well, when they showed up, I had the gift of the first book waiting for them as well as a document with the "Unveiled Book Club" clearly outlined and the heart behind it described. Each of them was giddy and grateful. What I learned by being obedient and reaching out to Jenni, Mary, and Nancy was that each of them was just waiting for a phone call from someone. All were looking for a deeper relationship with other women who would encourage them to seek a relationship with God and a deeper understanding of Him. I can't tell you how scared I was to initiate that book club. But now I can't imagine having missed out on great relationships with these now treasured friends.

All right, Mom, pom-poms up! Take the initiative! Sit down and make a list of friends or acquaintances you might like to spend more intentional time with, and then consider what that might look like. Ideas are easy; bringing them to fruition takes effort and guts. Be that woman who makes it happen! Be mindful of women who would have the availability or who have children close to your children's ages so you can have them play together while you chat.

Or consider those who would allow you to meet up at a local library, park, church playground, or even a fast-food playground. Think outside the box and see if you can make this work for a special group of moms you know. God made us for relationship with Him and with others who help strengthen our relationship with Him. Be proactive and reach out to other women to form real relationships that will challenge you and draw you closer to Him.

Substitute BFF

If you're lacking in friendships with other moms, be leery of a tendency to seek out friendship with your children in an unhealthy and counterproductive way. In an effort to be liked by their children, parents can cause the line between parenting and friendship to get blurred to the point where decisions about what's best for a child are tossed aside. Instead, remaining a friend becomes a priority, and giving the child whatever he or she wants is the goal.

Rather than filling the role of mom, you morph into trying to be your child's BFF—best friend forever. Being your child's friend in a mutually satisfying sort of way needs to be reserved for when he or she is older. While your children are living under your roof and are under your authority, you need to parent first.

This desire to be liked by one's children and their friends can cause moms to do some pretty strange things—birthday parties that are over the top, lavish gifts, extravagant travel, and designer price tags on clothing. This odd behavior also manifests itself in the way a mom speaks and interacts with her children. It's as if being "one of the gang" and gaining acceptance trumps good parenting. All discussions become negotiations, and children figure out quickly that playing on Mom's need to be liked can afford them some extra bargaining power.

Allow me to remind you, and myself: Our children have plenty of friends, but they only have one mom. Be the mom. You can still be the Fun Mom, but don't allow the need for friendship to turn your child into a meism monster. My friend Barbara Rainey puts it this way:

> Parents must love their children enough to say no when it's necessary. Parenting is not a political campaign or a popularity contest. "No" is a very powerful and important word, if you want to shepherd your children safely through the growing-up years.[3]

If you have a habit of giving your children whatever they want, you may be creating an expectation that may just stick with them the rest of their lives. I have seen this happen, especially in girls. I've seen them come home crying because once they got married, they weren't getting the "Yes, whatever you want dear!" they had become accustomed to receiving from their parents.

Mom, if you overdo it by paying for your daughter to have manicures and pedicures, hair treatments, or frequent trips to the local mall, you may be setting her future husband up for some rough times, and no mom wants to do that. In our efforts to pro-

mom truth

○○○○○○○○○○○○○○○○○○○○○○○○

How I see myself and relate to the women around me can have a profound effect on how I parent my children and model relationship to them. Accepting who God has made you to be and not comparing yourself with others, or altering who you are for the approval of others (even your own children), will allow you to love others and yourself more fully.

vide for our daughters out of love, we may instead be instilling expectations that aren't realistic. When you do choose to do something extravagant for your daughter, explain it as just that, and make it for special occasions only—even if you could afford to do it more frequently.

Parents also need to be mindful of ways they give in to their boys' wants and desires. Some boys can easily spend hours doing what they like, such as playing video games, participating in sports, watching YouTube videos, going to sporting events, or engaging in various other activities. Each of these things in moderation might be okay for your son, but it's important that he learn the discipline of setting limits. His future wife isn't going to appreciate a husband who disconnects from home life for hours on end on a regular basis.

Every child is different, so these scenarios may look different for your children. But the basic premise is that every child's expectations for what others will do for him or her later in life are being groomed now. Anticipate areas you see that could be potential problems for them in the future. Think through how you can model good behavior patterns and instill in your child the ability to have realistic and appropriate expectations.

On Sunday nights in our home, we share what each of us has planned or would like to plan for the next week. We sync up our calendars because knowing ahead of time helps us have similar expectations. We know who's doing what, who's going where, who's coming over, and so on. This is a learned habit that we think will serve our kids well in future relationships.

Also, in an effort to give my children a word picture when they get too inwardly focused, I ask them if they are getting dizzy. Because obviously, since they think the world is revolving around them, all that spinning must be making them dizzy! They grin and shake their heads. They know what I mean. My dizzy comment is my humorous way of reminding them of the harsh truth that they won't always get their way in life. And that's okay.

○　○　○

Our ability to be content shouldn't be based on comparisons of what others have. The Mirror Mom trap goes back to the question the wicked queen asked of the mirror in the first place: "Who is the fairest one of all?" The fact is that in our own lives, we should never look to the mirror for our self-worth. The Bible has an amazing truth to tell us: "Charm is deceptive, and beauty is fleeting; but a woman who fears the LORD is to be praised" (Proverbs 31:30).

Remember, Mom, God has uniquely fashioned you. The mirror doesn't determine your value. Allow me to assure you that once you figure that out, the mirror offers no questions. You can grin at the mirror and find much-needed peace in your reflection.

Mirror-Mom-Trap Quiz

Please read the following statements and rate yourself on a scale from
one (strongly agree) to five (strongly disagree). Then answer the corresponding questions or follow the instructions.

1. I am content with my lifestyle and life choices, and I am
   not tempted to try measuring up to those around me
   who appear to have it better than I do. _____

   Make a list of all the things you have to be grateful for—
   you'll need a notebook to list them all!

2. As I look at what matters in life, I believe I do have the
   ideal life. _____

   Confess in writing things you have coveted in others, and
   seek forgiveness from the Lord.

3. I am quick to overlook offenses and forgive people I feel have wronged me. _____

   Think of times when you have felt slighted by those around you or have easily taken offense and felt hurt or left out. (If sharing aloud with others, don't mention names.) Take an honest look at your sensitivities, and forgive the people you are harboring resentment or hurt feelings toward.

4. I have a relationship with someone (such as an accountability partner) who speaks truth into my life—even the hard truth. _____

   Make a list of women you could potentially seek out to have this kind of relationship with, and pray for the courage to make those calls.

5. I find parenting more important than friendship with my children, even if it means being unpopular with them. _____

Make a two-column list; record areas where you have set limits with your children and areas where you have overindulged them. What does your list reveal?

Scoring Chart

  5–8 = You are comfortable looking in the mirror and are able to accept who you are without shame or pride.

  9–12 = You are comfortable with the reflection you see in the mirror, but you do have some unnecessary self-talk occurring.

13–16 = The mirror and the pull to be accepted by and measure up to those around you is beginning to be reflected in your thoughts and attitudes.

17–20 = You are dangerously close to being trapped; you need to change course.

21–25 = You are gripped by the Mirror Mom trap, and you need to break free.

Next Up . . .

Have you ever heard women say such things as, "Oh, I miss my son being a little baby; he just got too big, too fast," or "I miss the cute toddler stage when my daughter loved to be laughed with and cuddled, and I was her favorite person in the whole world"? As moms, we find that each day provides opportunities to speak into our children's lives, but sadly our children seem to grow up all too fast. The inability to recognize that the clock is ticking daily and time is slipping away is something I refer to as the Tomorrow Mom trap. In the next chapter, we'll discover how we can live life intentionally!

CHAPTER 7

Tomorrow Mom Trap

Tomorrow is another day.

Even though the movie seemed ancient, as a teenager I was completely enthralled by *Gone with the Wind*. So much so that I devoured every chapter in the book, which was filled with real-life emotion tucked into one of the most tumultuous times in American history—the Civil War. I remember while watching the movie that I fully embraced the epic Scarlett O'Hara line, "After all, tomorrow is another day."

Throughout the years, on more than one occasion I have uttered that line, not as a declaration for intended future accomplishment, but as a cop-out because I had more to face than I was willing to deal with—and I liked the spunk Scarlett embodied. Sort of an "I'll get it done one of these days; don't bug me now," head-cocked-sideways, eyebrow-up attitude. I'm guessing you, like me, may have embraced that testy attitude once or twice yourself! The truth is that we've all had those moments where it just doesn't feel like there are enough hours in the day to get everything done.

Today Matters

Have you ever felt like all you do is "mother"? Have you ever felt as if that's all you'll ever do? Let's do some addition together, shall we?

My children are three years apart. I started parenting in my home in 1993, and I will cease parenting in my home around 2014. So that's twenty-one years of parenting. The average person lives eighty years; however, I intend to be far superior in that endeavor, so let's say one hundred. (C'mon, how cool would it be to live to be one hundred?) That means that of my one hundred years, I'll parent only 20 percent of my life. I have only twenty-one years to empower my children to live meaningful lives and make a difference in this world.

Once our children hit those tween years, they're much less interested in our influence, so we want to imprint as much as we can on them by the time they reach puberty. We want to lay a firm foundation when our children are young, so they'll be confident to stand for what's right, even if they have to stand alone.

In his book *Generation iY*, Tim Elmore reveals the following statistics about the generation born between 1990 and 2002 (Generation iY): "My research tells me [these young people] typically spend over 50 percent of their day with peers and only 15 percent with adults, including parents. In fact, 30 percent of their day is spent without any adult supervision."[1]

Once teens get their driver's license, parents typically see them less and less. And by eighteen, they are often out of the home. So now we're talking meaningful parenting for less than 20 percent of our lives!

Hit with these realities, "After all, tomorrow is another day" suddenly sounds rather fleeting. Could it be that *today* is the day? I can tell you this: I am amazed by the reality that my children are teenagers. Time has flown by. And the questions that ring through my ears are, *Have I been intentional enough in preparing them for the future? Has the illusion of permanence caused me to miss out on relationship with my children? Have parenting opportunities slipped by due to my "I have time tomorrow" mentality?*

Almost. But not quite. My husband and I recognized the illusion while our children were in elementary school. During a family vacation, we looked at each other and asked, "How did they grow up so fast?" Vacations have a way of doing that to you, because day after day, you may not necessarily notice the changes in your children, but on vacation, when what was fun last year is too "little kid" this year, you see it.

We used to go with my husband's family to a beach house in South Carolina every year, and one of our traditions was to boogie-board. My husband was usually with my daughter, and I was usually with my son, and we helped them out and cheered them on. This particular year, they let us know that they didn't need our help; they were fine on their own.

I remember dragging our beach chairs down to the water's edge, to be within leaping distance, if necessary. And as Bill and I sat there watching them play with each other and successfully catch waves all on their own, we realized we had turned a corner. Sure, over the past several months, things had occurred that indicated their independence and capacity to do more for themselves. But at that moment, comparing the past year with what we were seeing, we realized that our children were growing up fast.

Bill and I joined our children in the ocean, but rather than helping them like we did when they were "little kids" (to quote my daughter), we were now just playing with them and having fun together. At times, we even wandered and separated from them (always with an eye on them, of course) to help them gain confidence and independence. Sort of like giving a horse his head with the reins—you're still in control; the horse just doesn't realize it.

Helicopter, Free Range, or Intentional

We have all heard about the two extremes of helicopter parents who hover and won't let children do their own thing, and free-range parents who turn them loose and don't get involved at all. For Bill and me, our parenting style was to avoid both extremes; instead, we took the positive attributes of both styles and intentionally parented our children so we could grow in relationship with them.

What did this look like for us? In daily life around our home, we gave our children more responsibilities and opportunities for growth and failure. They learned from their mistakes. Remember, they're making pots.

When motherhood started for me, I guess I had the ridiculous thought that I had all the time in the world. As long as I pedaled hard enough on occasion, I could let go of the handlebars, throw my arms out to the side, and coast, right? Not so much. I have now come to realize that a slow, steady pedaling, with hands gently grasping the handlebars, will allow a smooth ride and make my journey much more satisfying. Especially when I hit the occasional momlife pebble!

Always putting off doing the right thing until tomorrow, or trying to coast through parenthood, robs us of the joy of building relationships with our children. Personal growth for children and their parents is obtained through daily intentional parenting. Remember that any child in your life is longing to matter, and taking the time to be intentional with your children inspires self-confidence in their young spirits.

Of the two extremes, I fear one of the negative outcomes of a free-range parenting style is that parents lose connection with their children. You can't speak into the life of a person with whom you have no relational equity. Conversely, the negative outcome of helicopter parenting is children who are paralyzed by indecision, poor self-confidence, and fear of the unknown, because they haven't learned to think for themselves.

I'm not saying that every minute of your life has to be spent with your children. There's a difference between the need to encourage your children to explore their independence during alone time and a lack of parental guidance. Free-range parenting gone amuck leads to ill-equipped children and peer-taught children, but it can be a tempting approach for an overwhelmed mom and dad, because it's less time consuming.

Motherhood does at times leave us yearning for some space, silence, and invisibility! I get it; I've been there. I know the question you wonder silently every day: *Will I get a chance today to go to the bathroom . . . alone?*

It's ironic that when our children are babies, we as parents get very little sleep because we're providing for their physical needs. During that stage, figuring out what those needs are can be challenging.

As our children become toddlers, they become much more vocal about their needs, and they try our patience with every excuse known to man that would allow them to stay up just a little later. Have you ever said, "I just wish they would be quiet, leave me alone, and go to sleep!"?

However, as they get a little older, especially when they reach the tween and teen stages, our challenge is to get some words, any words, out of them. To actually elicit dialogue, you must skillfully fish for even a morsel of information. My children are at that stage now, and I've learned that I must make myself available to talk whenever and wherever the mood to talk strikes them—morning, noon, or night.

Sadly, some parents spend their children's younger years wearing themselves out, seeing to every need to keep their little ones happy and not whining. Then when their children get to the stage where they begin to pull back, the parents welcome the change with relief and let them wander off alone, free-range style. Some intentionally, some accidentally. But here's what you need to remember: When your children lose your influence, they become influenced by whatever relationships or activities they find to replace you, whether peers, television, movies, the Internet, video games, coaches, teammates, or older siblings.

Your children will naturally find themselves out from under your influence soon enough. While you have the chance to be an involved, intentional mother, you should take the opportunity to do so. My mother used to advise me, "Tracey, don't wish your life away," because at each stage of my life, I was impatient for the next stage. Mom, I implore you to enjoy each stage of your child's life and not be a victim of the Tomorrow Mom trap.

Relationship Matters

I think one of the biggest problems in parenting today is that parents have gotten away from simple family time together. If you make family time a habit when your children are young and stick to it as they mature, it really just becomes part of the way your family does life.

Helicopter parents spend time with their children, but they do so by hovering over them and dictating what they can and cannot do. This can actually rob their children of the capacity to make their own decisions. I have heard it described as "cowboying" a child instead of shepherding. A cowboy pushes; a shepherd leads. So here's what you should do: Instead of holding on too tight and pushing, as your children get older, let go of different areas and allow them to make age-appropriate decisions. Guide them and lead them in such a way that they can learn to problem-solve for themselves.

Teachers understand that the most valuable assets a student can have are the ability to be teachable, or led, and a desire to learn. By transferring a teachable spirit into the lives of your children at home, you give them the opportunity to grow, learn, and experience new things. How do you do this? You might let them go on well-chaperoned trips with family, friends, or church groups. This allows them to experience freedom in safe settings with safe people, so they can learn independence.

You can create opportunities in your own home that allow your children to learn to be problem solvers. Our son wanted to build a tree house, and rather than my husband taking over the project, he provided our son with boards, hammers, nails, and an offering of minimal assistance. Did it turn out to be an amazing tree-house structure? Not really, but our son gained confidence and subsequently remained interested in doing projects.

One of the saddest displays of parents taking over and doing things for their kids rather than allowing them to do for themselves reveals itself every year during science fairs. We've lived in several different communities, and I've seen it in all of them. You probably have too. Do me a favor; let your child do his or her own school projects. The science fair is for the students, not the parents! (I hope you're laughing; I am because it's so true and so silly!)

A very good daily opportunity to build a relationship with your children is around the breakfast table and/or the dinner table. We try to eat dinner together at home every night, and our children know they're going to hear their dad say, "Tell me one thing about your day today." This leads to some serious conversation, some silly conversation, and some eye-opening conversation on exactly what goes on during our children's days at school.

One night at dinner, my daughter was clearly exasperated with our ineptness as adults, parents, and humans because we weren't seeing things her way. To defuse the situation, my brilliant husband uttered the following: "Did you know that when teenagers turn fifteen, they emit a chemical that eliminates all brain capacity of their parents? Really, the parents lose the ability to think rationally."

My daughter was all over that; she readily agreed and said, "I believe it! That's so true!" Then my husband added, "And you know what else? They emit that same chemical at school, and the same thing happens to all the teachers!" Immediately, she shouted, "Yes, I knew it!" And we ended our meal laughing and poking fun at each other. This could have become a volatile conversation, but because of years of spending time together and building relationship, Bill used a little humor to deal with the situation.

Of course, we recognize what's going on here: We want control, and our daughter wants independence. So we have to use relationship and love to get through the process successfully.

So what does relationship look like? I think it looks like not taking yourself too seriously but instead having fun with your children as you do life together. Small acts of entering their worlds show them that you love them and that you can be trusted.

One of my son's favorite things has always been cars. From the time he was very young, he would see a car drive by and name the make, model, and year. I always thought it was rather strange; to me a car is just a way to get from point A to point B. But because he liked them, we read books about cars, went to car shows, played with Hot Wheels cars, watched television shows about cars—you get the idea. I asked all kinds of questions just to show interest. This allowed him to be the expert on something and teach me! It would have been easier to leave him to explore such things himself, but engaging with him grew our relationship.

Entering our children's worlds needs to start early and continue until . . . well, I'm not sure, 'cause I'm still doin' it!

One of my children's favorite things in the world used to be doing errands with me. Why? Because if they were well mannered and helpful, the very last thing we would do was take a trip to the toy store. They could go wherever they wanted, and I would follow and ooh and aah. We always left empty-handed; we weren't there to buy, just to play! Brilliant, I know. Who needs theme parks? Yes, going to the toy store added an extra stop, but it went a long way toward allowing my children some "lead" time in our relationship, which built confidence.

Connecting with your children doesn't just have to be all fun and games. You can have family time getting those home-improvement projects done, too. Our projects are usually a family affair, whether indoor or outdoor chores or special projects. We believe in the buddy system, because if at least one person is working with you, the job becomes a bonding experience. We do indoor chores with loud music playing, have water fights while we wash the cars, have acorn fights as we rake leaves, and even have lawn-mower races! Okay, that does sound like fun and games, doesn't it? But the work gets done too!

Intentional Togetherness

Being intentional about spending time together shouldn't just be reserved for the everyday. I would encourage you to spend special times together as well. Rather than something that separates you, find an activity that bonds you. Our family has always enjoyed camping. For a while there, we went camping at least once a month as an intentional means of spending time together away from the noise of the world.

We asked the kids' soccer coaches, "Are you okay with our children being gone one weekend a month? If not, the kids won't be able to join the team." Every time we asked, the coaches agreed. Isn't that interesting? Stand your ground, parents of athletes! Do what's best for your family first!

Ever since our children were in the first grade, my husband has taken each of them away for a weekend every year. My husband and my daughter go to Pine Cove Christian Camps in Tyler, Texas, for father-daughter time in the spring, and he takes my son to camp for father-son time in the fall. Obviously, while one child is on this adventure with my husband, the other is at home with me. Great relationship and together time has occurred as a result of these special events, and we all look forward to them every year.

As the children have gotten older, we've found other special times together by going to college sporting events, concerts, and local parks; going on picnics, hiking trips, and day trips to state parks; attending car shows; and even going antiquing—you don't have to spend money to make memories. Yes, it's a bit of a hassle to pack up a cooler and venture out on a weekend when you could be relaxing at home, but as with anything else, once you actually do it, you want to do more of it!

I have a friend whose young son was enthralled with football and really wanted to learn how to play. His dad went online, got a flag-football team kit, and gathered a group of other dads to host a regular father-son, Saturday-morning flag-football game. The moms took turns sending snacks, and the dads taught their sons the finer points about football and had a little "life lesson" at the end of every game. Simple, practical, parent-involved fun and connecting!

A few years ago we started going with our daughter and two of her friends to a family-style, Saturday-night rodeo. There next to the rodeo arena sat three sets of parents, two of which had never set foot near a rodeo. This may not have been their personal first choice of how to spend a Saturday night, but entering into their daughters' worlds to intentionally connect was important.

You might find yourself doing some pretty crazy things with your children, but there's another bonus: It will keep you young! Have you ever seen one of those movies where the good guys are running from the bad guys through the woods, and the good guys burst through the woods, teeter on top of a cliff, and look down at the water below? Then comes the moment where the good guys must make that crazy decision: face the bad guys or jump to a possible painful death.

Oh yes I did! Minus the bad guys and the jog through the woods. I found myself standing at the top of a thirty-five-foot cliff looking down at a large body of water. Rather than facing bad guys, I was facing teenagers yelling, "C'mon, Mom! You can do it!" So I did it. And I liked it. I even did it several more times. Sideline Mom no more; you may call me Fun Mom!

If I think back to my childhood, I don't really remember much about the trip to Disney World, but I can give you vivid details of the times we went camping. Mom's tennis shoe melted because she was too close to the fire; Dad ran out of the woods because he was supposedly being chased by a bear; my sister, Shari, my brother, Bo, and I got lost hiking and were rescued by a park ranger; the tent froze, and the whole family huddled up together in our sleeping bags, laughing hysterically at the insanity of camping when it was so cold. Those memories with my family are forever etched in my heart.

Dennis and Barbara Rainey are the founders of FamilyLife, a marriage and family ministry that has been in existence for more than thirty years. Barbara has long told the story of how her daughter Rebecca was very involved in gymnastics. Barbara and Dennis began to recognize that Rebecca spent more time with her coach than with the family.

It was initially hard for Barbara and Rebecca to let go of the sport, but Dennis made the decision, and they agreed that it wasn't worth the cost of losing out on their relationship and the ability to daily speak into Rebecca's life. That decision cleared the way for more hang-out time. Looking back, all three are grateful for that decision.[2]

Children participating in sports programs isn't necessarily bad. I just think that spending exorbitant amounts of time in these programs can lead to isolation from the family, which ultimately leads to loss of relationship. Practice schedules eat into family time, and for this reason, many parents are choosing to allow their children to pick only one sport per season instead of several. If we teach our children to live with no time for family when they're young, it may be a habit they carry over into adulthood.

I have friends whose children decided to actually quit playing sports altogether because they were burned-out and weary and wanted to just live their lives. I'm not sure if it's because they never really wanted to play sports to begin with, or if it simply became too much. I do recognize that some children are gifted athletes, and if that is their natural bent, then support them in it and be their biggest fan! Just teach them good time management.

Relationship Earns You the Right to Teach

If you think Bill and I place too much emphasis on family bonding in our home, and you're wondering why we do all this bonding stuff, I'd like you to understand that if you work on having a good relationship with your children now, when something goes wrong and they make a mistake (which they will), or when they have problems (which they will), you will have earned the right to speak into their lives.

When our daughter was a tween, she went through a period when she and her father were having a power struggle, and that led to a power struggle with me, too. I cannot begin to tell you how many times the battle raged in our home, but it was enough that she was spending a lot of time arguing with us, and we were spending a lot of time with short fuses, wondering if we were officially the world's worst parents.

On one such occasion, while Mom and Dad were searching God's Word and seeking to be taught some lessons by Him, a lesson revealed itself in one word . . . *whatever*. Just how do we deal with the anger within our precious, prayed for, and prayed over daughter? It was after school one day when God's answer revealed itself fully. Allow me to take you there.

"Whatever." And the door slammed. I stood in amazement, staring at the wooden door inches from my nose. How could my sweet little girl have turned into this trite little eye-rolling creature that hurled hurtful words at me? Knowing that my age and experience would make me a sure winner, I was tempted to join in on a war of words with her. But I remembered that I was the adult, so I swallowed my pride, lifted up a quick prayer, and asked God to direct my next step.

I tried to put myself in my daughter's place and asked myself what could be the motive for this continual display of blatant disrespect. She knew better, and quite frankly, it was out of character for her. *Maybe it's adolescence. Maybe she's testing her boundaries. Or just maybe it's that she spends eight hours every day in an atmosphere where she is trying to maneuver her way into being accepted and valued,* I thought. *School can be tough.*

Regardless of why she was choosing to act that way, as a parent I needed to help her through it, not fight with her. I paused for a cooling-off period, then took a deep breath and decided, *I'm going in*. I knocked. A quiet voice mumbled, "Come in." My daughter looked up at me through those bangs that curl just a bit on each side of her big brown eyes, and I could see a look of curious apprehension. She knew she'd messed up, and she was waiting to see what her punishment would be.

"I've been hearing that word *whatever* from you a lot lately. The word itself isn't offensive; it's the way you say it. And what's with the door slam? We don't slam doors in this house," I said.

Her gentle voice, with a tinge of aggravation, replied, "I know. I just get so sick of you telling me what to do."

We spent the better part of the evening discussing how she could remember to complete her daily responsibilities without me constantly telling her what to do. We came up with a written reminder checklist and posted it on her bedroom door. That list would allow her to check her own progress throughout the day. We agreed that if she didn't accomplish her daily tasks, the consequence would be more chores. I wish I could say things went perfectly after that, but although things did get a lot better, we did (and sometimes still do) struggle with the completion of tasks and balancing the "to do" and the "to be." However, we made progress that day.

What was that other problem? Remember the "whatever" attitude? Our biggest discussion while sitting in that bedroom was about her attitude. Yes, she was having a hard time at school. Yes, there were cruelties and challenges, and we talked about how that was part of growing up. I assured her that I understood and I cared.

There was another item I posted on her door—something for her to memorize:

> Finally, brothers [and sisters], *whatever* is true, *whatever* is noble, *whatever* is right, *whatever* is pure, *whatever* is lovely, *whatever* is admirable—if anything is excellent or praiseworthy—think about such things. (Philippians 4:8, emphasis added)

For the next several weeks, every time she said "Whatever" to me, my daughter was asked to recite the verse aloud. I challenged her by suggesting that whenever she became frustrated or hurt and the word *whatever* popped into her mind, she should recite Philippians 4:8 in her head. Interestingly, God challenged me to do the same thing, so we ended up memorizing the verse together. In our home, "whatever" became a reminder that how we think is important, and when we turn over our issues to God, our attitudes become more loving.

Teachable moment, yes, but if I had lost my cool, no teaching would have occurred, just a downward spiral of hurt feelings and unmet expectations. Sometimes keeping our cool while parenting can be hard, but with God's help, we can do it.

Part of teaching our children includes teaching them the Word of God in practical, life-application ways. The tenser a situation is, the more we need the Word of God to guide us on how to handle it. Be creative and intentional, add a dose of humor or levity when possible, and model an approach to life you want your children to embrace.

During our daughter's high-school years, she made some choices we didn't agree with and those became opportunities to process life with her and help her grow in wisdom. When we could see that she was going off in a ditch, we would have some very serious conversations with her. Although she didn't always like to listen to us, she did. We had a relationship with her, and we had earned the right for her to listen to us. When put to the test, our strong-willed teenager sat down, spoke her mind, listened to our counsel, and was willing to be obedient to our authority. We weren't uninvolved parents suddenly trying to speak into her life; we were involved parents continuing to speak into her life. It makes a difference. We strived to point her to the One who had the answers and prayed she would hear His voice above all others.

Seek Help—or Offer It—When Needed

We, as moms, do so much for others that sometimes we find it difficult to ask for help ourselves when we need it. I think this mom trait is even more prominent in the lives of our single-mom friends out there. They need support from friends and coworkers who value their at-home role as much as their at-work role. When they don't receive that, the weight of both roles begins to wear them down.

If there is a single mom in your life, ask her how you can help. And if you're a single mom, I encourage you to ask others for help. Sometimes it just takes someone to make that first step for a mutually rewarding relationship to blossom. Take that first step, Mom! Time goes by quickly, and you could be making a difference in a single mom's life right now.

I have heard from more than one single mom that one of the biggest unmet needs single moms experience is finding a strong male role model to speak into the lives of their sons. For many of these single moms, their sons' fathers are out of the picture. The question is, Are there other men who could step into the lives of these young men and help out?

In today's busy world, when dads struggle to find enough time for their own families, I think the last thought on their minds is to reach out to a child who doesn't have a father in his life. That unmet need is simply not on most men's radar screens.

What I would like to suggest to my married sisters out there is that you consider whether your husband could fill that role in the life of a young man. No doubt you know a single mom with a son who is longing to spend time with a man—maybe your man.

Mentoring young men has been a part of my husband's life for several years. Currently Bill meets regularly with an older teenage boy who comes to his office after school. My husband and my son have breakfast weekly with one of my son's friends. For each of these young men, having a man who is interested and available to talk about "guy stuff" has been a real blessing. As a result, this has taught our son the importance of reaching out and making a difference in the lives of others.

If you and your husband decide to reach out to a boy or a young man, you should set some boundaries. Make certain they meet in areas where others are always around. And you should reach out and befriend the single mom (if you don't know her already). Be the one to make the phone calls to set up the times together and initiate the contact. That just makes good sense.

Wisdom Matters

As my oldest was entering her teen years, my husband and I were blessed to be part of a group made up of several couples who had children older than ours. They, like us, were chasing hard after knowledge from God's Word on how to live life well and leave a strong legacy. We helped graduate, marry, and give baby showers to the children of these dear friends. The up-close look at them launching their children caused us to become very aware of the illusion of permanence.

I have asked other parents older and wiser than I, with children older than mine, what advice they would give on how to successfully raise children who can manage on their own. When I met Karen Loritts, I had this compulsion to sort of follow her around in hopes that some of her would rub off on me. For more than thirty-seven years, Karen has labored alongside her husband, Crawford, a pastor, and has poured her life into other women through teaching, public speaking, and serving in her community. While doing so, she raised four children who continue to be committed to Christ and use their lives to serve others. She has a thing or two to share with us about training up children in the way they should go (Proverbs 22:6):

> While raising our children, we faced the usual challenges with
> siblings bickering, sloppiness with household chores, and
> working long hours on school assignments. We taught them
> how to build meaningful and lasting friendships, even how to

cope with neighborhood bullies. There were many discussions about being dependable and faithful and being kind to one another. Such words as *love, diligence, kindness,* and *integrity* were used a lot. Our intention was to inspire good character without nagging or seeming to brainwash them. We honestly wanted our children to embrace good character. We prayed for wisdom.[3]

Without exception, parents who have blazed the trail ahead of us have told my husband and me that we must make an effort to spend quality time with our children while also being willing to *let go* of our children, a little bit at a time. They've encouraged us to allow our children to try things on their own, succeed on their own, and fail on their own. We need to cheer them on for trying and succeeding, but more important, teach them how to recover from their failures.

A father a few years ahead of us in the parenting journey advised us to intentionally (there's that word again) give up one or two "big" things each year that our children could become responsible for on their own. We started with personal-hygiene responsibilities (dressing themselves, choosing their clothes, brushing their teeth, and so on), and then with chores and responsibilities around the house (helping out with washing dishes, taking out the trash, vacuuming, etc.). And now we're into money management, schoolwork, time management, and giving to others.

Realize that you're not seeking perfection in teaching the virtue of responsibility. What you are doing is training. When a responsibility isn't met, you discuss with your children the consequences of failing to meet their own set standards and enable them to learn from their failures. Eventually they slowly (emphasis on *slowly*) live up to their own expectations of themselves. In doing so, they teach themselves without your breathing down their necks and becoming a nag. (I speak from personal experience on that nag thing.)

Our friends Barry and Sandra shared with us that by the time their children were seniors in high school, they had set their own curfews and were simply asked to call if they were going to be late. The result: Their kids learned before they went to college (and were still in the safety of their parents' home) how to set a curfew for themselves, and that when they were late, they suffered at school the next day. This may not work for your family, but you can find ways to shift certain responsibilities and decisions to your kids.

If you've never thought of what it's going to be like when your children go off to college, now may be a good time to do just that. What is an involved, fun-loving mom to do when faced with that reality? Well, actually, she is to get her little self prepared for the inevitable. That's why I so appreciate the book *Barbara and Susan's Guide to the Empty Nest*.

Barbara and Susan helped me understand that I need to start planning now for my empty nest. Not that I need to do anything earth-shattering; I simply need to consider all options through the

mom truth ○○○○○○○○○○○○○○○○○○○○○

At times, the demands of being a mom can overwhelm me and tempt me to put things off until tomorrow, never realizing that this mind-set can lead to apathy and missed opportunities. Remember, Mom, your children are merely on loan to you for a short time, and today their needs and your relationship with them is paramount. To earn the right to speak into their lives, you need to make relationship a priority by being an intentional mom and raising your children for true greatness.

lens of "What is important right now, while our children are still in our home?" "Am I preparing them for true greatness?" This mothering thing is all about preparing these people for the world and being ready to let go when the time comes. The scary part is making sure you've prepared them well for their future.

As I contemplated the future of my someday empty nest, my sadness was replaced with anticipation of all the memories we can make between now and then. It also caused me to consider what God may have for me to do once my little ones have flown! Now, instead of looking toward the empty nest with dread and fear, I'm learning to look with expectancy and excitement.

Moms, one day soon, far sooner than you want to admit, those children will fly from your nest, and your gift from God, of time spent with them daily, will vanish. Poof! (Of course, children don't disappear entirely.) Something tells me (actually many someones who have lived it tell me) that when that happens, you'll jump at the chance to giggle through an evening with a toddler, stay up late talking to a teen, or stand over a bed in prayer for a sleeping child.

Whenever I grow weary of the daily grind with my children and have the thought, *I'll do it tomorrow*, or *I can't wait till they're out of here!* God brings to mind the Tomorrow Mom trap and cautions me not to wish my life away too soon. He still has much for me to teach my children before they fly the nest!

Tomorrow-Mom-Trap Quiz

Please read the following statements and rate yourself on a scale from one (strongly agree) to five (strongly disagree). Then answer the corresponding questions or follow the instructions.

1. I "get" that time is fleeting and that my tomorrows are slipping away. I am intentional with my relationships with my children. _____

   Ask each of your children to spend an afternoon with you doing whatever they want to do! Get it on the calendar!

2. I work to intentionally parent my children toward independence. _____

   Do you lean toward the free-range parenting style or the helicopter parenting style? What could you do differently to be more of an intentional parent?

3. I make time for my children and do activities they prefer with them. _____

   Make a list of activities you could do with each of your children to connect around their natural "bent."

4. My relational equity with my children has been a priority, and I do speak into their lives. _____

   Jot down some ideas of a possible day trip or overnight trip you could take with each of your children to work toward a special connection.

5. I have older, wiser parents in my life whom I seek advice and experiential knowledge from. _____

Whom could you go to for godly wisdom on child rearing? (Hint: Ask those whose children exhibit godly character qualities, especially when no one is looking.)

Scoring Chart

  5–8 = You intentionally spend quality time with your children and are growing in your relationship with them, which allows open communication.

  9–12 = You have a good relationship with your children, but you could be more intentional in pouring time and wisdom into their lives.

13–16 = You are trying to connect with your children but are permitting a bit too much distance, by choice or circumstance; either way, look for a solution.

17–20 = You are dangerously close to being trapped; you need to change course.

21–25 = You are in the Tomorrow Mom trap, and you are desperate for rescue.

Next Up . . .

The world seems to help lay out before us the Mirror Mom trap and the Tomorrow Mom trap, but then it goes one step further and muddles our thought lives with the messages we constantly hear from others, which brings us to the They Say Mom trap. Let's tackle this one together!

CHAPTER 8

They Say Mom Trap

You know what they say!

How can you be the mom you want to be, and the mom you think God wants you to be, when the voices all around you are screaming at you constantly, and all have differing opinions?

There's a standing joke in my family that whenever my mother imparts wisdom based on something she's heard, it usually starts with the phrase "Well, now, they say . . ." We always reply, "Just who are 'they,' and why do we care what they say?" I have a sneaking suspicion that you've probably heard others say this to you, or maybe you've said it yourself. There seem to be a lot of "theys" doing a lot of saying!

My caution to you, Mom, is don't live your life based on what "they say," or you'll be buried up to your neck in the They Say Mom trap. For those of you who struggle with the voices of others, or have friends who do, please learn from my experience that standing against the They Say Mom trap is doable and empowering as a God-thinking mom.

The Talk

As moms, we now have bombarding us daily the voices of lots and lots of "theys" through the power of the Internet and social media. Add to that the numerous television hosts who spout what society and psychologists and their perceived majority say regarding how we should all be living, and you end up with enough opinions to muddle anyone's brain.

Today, more than at any other time in history, moms have myriad choices on how they can spend the hours of their day. Electronics and gadgets that maximize efficiency allow us to multitask like never before. There are work-outside-the-home moms, work-inside-the-home moms, and stay-at-home moms. Each group of moms has thoughts and opinions on why their way of living is best, and each group has sisters alongside them heralding their beliefs.

In fact, I would like to propose a new way of looking at and referring to ourselves as moms. No more references to SAHMs, WAHMs, and working moms. We're all moms and we all work. The pivotal question is, Where are we placing our priorities in daily life as we do the work we've been called to do? We are all MWWs: moms who work. None of us is more important than the other; what *is* important is that we make the people and relationships in our homes our first priority.

The truth is that choices in today's environment leave us all feeling pulled in so many directions that we can end up twisted in a knot like a pretzel. Even the choices we encounter while grocery shopping can fill us with confusion. The money, time, and effort spent on marketing to convince us which choice to make could probably run a small country! With all these options, we often look to other voices to tell us what's best for our families and us.

We don't know which choice to make, so we ask those around us what cereal they eat, what gifts they're getting their children, what sports their children are going to play, and where they're planning to go on vacation. Then we figure that their choices should be our choices, too. At face value, that approach may be easier—the whole go-with-the-flow idea—but it lacks wisdom.

Listening to the "they say" choices usually requires us to spend more money than we should on stuff we don't need, and more time doing things we weren't necessarily intended to do. The needs to fit in and do as others do are the teeth of the They Say Mom trap that grab hold of us tightly.

I've received an alarming number of questions on my Web site from moms who seem to question their own judgment regarding what's best for their children (and themselves) because they feel pressure to do what the rest of the crowd is doing. Even when these moms indicate that they intuitively know what the right choice is, they need reassurance that their own instincts are correct. Moms in the They Say Mom trap can become paralyzed by in-decision or lulled into complacency by doing what others say instead of what they know is best for their children, their family, and themselves.

It certainly is evident that what "they say" is steering too many parents and children in the wrong direction. The world is trying to turn children into little adults. We see it in clothing choices, the electronics our children carry around, the media choices they are exposed to, and even in the number of hours each day when they are "scheduled" to do something. What scares me most is that going along with what "they say" can create stressed-out, performance-driven children.

Somebody please stop the madness! We need to slow down and remember what being a mom, and being a kid, is all about.

What Matters Most

I cringe when I hear a mom say, "My kids are driving me crazy! I cannot wait to get out of this house." And they do say that . . . a lot. I've said it. Here are a few lamentations that have come out of my mouth: "I am so sick of this I could scream!" "Sweatpants and bedroom slippers again—how pathetic am I?" And "I'm so tired; I wish I could escape somewhere!"

Ahem . . . Has anyone besides me joined the "they say" voices by doing a lot of complaining about the hard work involved in being a mom? Seeing motherhood as being trapped in the house with the kids? Maybe you're attempting to keep up with the Joneses, maybe you want to have more excitement or just do something different, anything just to get out of the house. Here's the thing to remember, Mom: It's not just a house; it's *your home*. There will be days when you're tired of refereeing the kids, eating PB&J sandwiches, and being the temperature gauge in the home. Expect those moments but know where your mind needs to go when that happens.

Remember, all moms have those other MOMents, too. You know the ones—those "My heart aches because I love my little one so much" moments. Moments you cannot fully comprehend or understand until you are a mom.

When I first became a mom, I had an overwhelming feeling of increased love. I thought I had understood God's love before, but I didn't fully understand it until I was holding that tiny little creation who had been fearfully and wonderfully made by Him.

That feeling of love can sneak up on you in your daily momlife, and it's one of the most amazing blessings of motherhood. Through your children, God gives you glimpses of Himself and His bountiful, unconditional love.

It may be your daughter's giggle or that shrill, cascading belly laugh that resonates from her as pure joy and that you receive as the reverberation of love. Sometimes it's your son's little hand that reaches over and clutches yours, so sweetly and gently, and as you look down into his sparkling eyes, he looks up into yours with the truth of love. Unconditional-to-the-core love for you, because you are mom. That kind of love breeds security and contentment in a child.

I have a very vivid memory of my son at about age eight. We were having dinner together as a family, all sitting around the kitchen table. We were talking, laughing, just doing life. Then he stood up, put one arm around his dad's neck and the other arm around my neck, turned and looked at his dad, then turned and looked at me, smiled that little boy smile, and said, "I love my life!"

As he sat back down, my husband and I locked eyes, and it was as if nothing else in the world mattered. All that truly did matter was *us*, together as a family, growing in relationship with one another and with God.

More recently with my teenage daughter, I regularly receive notes in which she sweetly recounts memories and showers me with words of appreciation. Not because we've lived without conflict but because we've intentionally worked at a strong parent-child relationship.

I wonder, what are your memories-of-love MOMents with your children? Those times when their love for you radiates through you and fills you with the joy of being their mom. Would you take the time right now to jot down some of your moments (right in the margins of this book, if you have to)?

We all have these moments—some are tender, some are silly. Quite honestly, I could fill, and have filled, pages with stories of special moments with my children. And you know what, I wouldn't trade those moments for anything in the entire world.

Ask any mom who's lost a child what she wouldn't give for more tender moments. After all, more than anything, isn't loving your children what you want to do and what they need from you? The next time you find yourself surrounded by voices complaining about motherhood, be intentional about not joining in. Be the one who looks for the positive.

When you're in the trenches of mothering, sometimes you can miss out on the special moments because the needs and demands of the day trump the sweetness of what being a mom is all about.

The truth of the matter is that we would all like our momlife a whole lot better if we had more MOMents and less of the messy, hard, draining, tiring, struggling-to-keep-my-sanity times of the day. We need to seek out those special moments. They will fill our hearts, and our children's hearts, with joy and the strength to keep going on difficult days.

You may have jotted down several MOMents earlier, but if you're realizing that those moments are becoming few and far between, it's time to make a change. Keep reading. We're in this together, Mom.

Where Do We Start?

God instructs us to be in the world but not of the world. The world tells us that to have great moments with our children, we need to buy them more stuff, provide them with a bigger house, drive a really cool car, go on big vacations, push them to make perfect grades, involve them in many activities. That's what "they say" will make them, and us, happy, and happiness is what we all deserve.

But wait, *we* are moms. We know that what will make our children contented, at peace, and able to become what God intends them to become is simply *love*—those love-filled moments when we get a soothing glimpse of God's love and His glory.

The idea that if you, and your children, do more, have more, and achieve more, then you and your children will be happy, and that's what you're intended to be—it's just not true. Simply put, you are being influenced into chasing after the things of this world, not the things of God. It's hard to model not placing value on "stuff and status," but we need to point our children in the opposite direction—placing value on relationships.

Dear sweet Mom, don't let the They Say Mom trap get its vice-like grip on you, for if it does, it can easily be handed down to your children. Being trapped in the They Say Mom trap makes the pace of life so out of control that we, and our children, end up drowning in a sea of performance-based love and stressful living. How can we escape or avoid this trap? It starts in the choices we make in our own homes and for our own families.

Allow me to share with you my daughter's favorite Bible verse:

> Do not conform any longer to the pattern of this world, but be
> transformed by the renewing of your mind. Then you will be
> able to test and approve what God's will is—his good, pleasing
> and perfect will. (Romans 12:2)

This is my daughter's favorite verse because she gets that not conforming to the world is a constant battle. Her mother gets that too, and getting that is a step toward battling it.

As moms, we sometimes get it wrong. When we feel unsure or insecure, we look to our right and our left to figure out how to live our lives. We've listened to far too many sentences that start with "Well, they say . . ." The problem with listening to what "they say" is that sometimes the "theys" doing the saying aren't living their lives from a biblical worldview. And many of us who claim to have a biblical worldview have been influenced by the ways of the world, and we've fallen away from God's intention for the family.

Once I began to read and really study the Bible, the theme that jumped out at me more than any other is that God truly intends for me to live a selfless life, practicing agape love, which is, by definition, selfless love (1 Corinthians 13:4-13). Our lives are to bring glory to God, and our model of how to do that is the life of Jesus Christ (Philippians 2:1-18). Jesus was completely selfless, to the point of death. I think the problem is that we've read these verses so often, we fail to let their truth sink in: We are to be selfless in our daily life.

Wow, God . . . really? That's hard; I mean crazy hard.

Then there's what "they say" that counters the truth: "You were put on this earth to be happy and fulfilled; do what's best for you." I admit it, my ears like that better. But if I believe that the Bible provides truth and that I'm supposed to apply that truth to my life, then—though it may seem countercultural—I must make selfless decisions. Believe me, I know this isn't easy, and I fail continually. But God has this way of reminding me that He can be the mom through me, if I allow Him to be.

The Mom Choice

Here's the central concern with the choices we all make every day: Do I do what God says, or do I do what "they say"? God's way is always going to be what's best for you and those entrusted to you. It's not always easy, but He will enable you. I promise. *He* promises. In Matthew 6:33, Jesus said, "But seek first [God's] kingdom and his righteousness, and all these things will be given to you as well." Ask yourself, "What am I seeking?"

In previous chapters, we've gotten some glimpses into how the They Say Mom trap can influence our thinking regarding our children. We allow our children to be overly involved in sports, gaming, or the latest social-media fad because others are letting their children do them. We're sacrificing what we know is best in the hope that our children will fit in.

We've also been reminded that listening to what "they say" can influence how we see ourselves. What will "they say" about me if I don't look as if I just stepped out of a magazine? If I'm not a part of every committee? If my home isn't spotless? We rob time that could be spent doing what matters with our children and having peace in our homes in order to manufacture the right look, the perfect house, or the perfect linen closet.

Some of us also need to consider the amount of time we spend pursuing our personal careers and aspirations, even our hobbies. What starts off as just a job can become something that steals us away from our children. In an interview I was doing with a young mom, she told me that she was raised believing that to have value, she had to have a job outside the home. I heard that same "I have to have a job" answer from several other young women. Their decision was based on the "they says" in their lives.

Do your hobbies and interests—yes, even social media—steal you away from your family? I encourage you to take a look at your schedule. Are there areas that need to be trimmed so that you can have more quality time with your children? Be intentional about your priorities. Write them down and then create your schedule around what's most important to you. What choices have you made because "they say" this is what you should do?

No matter the voices you have heard whispering in your ear, I want you to be encouraged and emboldened, Mom! You can ignore those voices and break free from the They Say Mom trap.

Moving Forward

As a mom who lives her life based on the "Here's what God says" grid, I choose to turn a deaf ear to "they" and seek God's thoughts on the matter. My life experience and the experiences of other moms with grown children have some telling similarities that offer enlightenment on the importance of mom and whom she listens to daily. Remember, our children are learning from us. If we constantly succumb to the pressure of what "they say," we're not teaching our children to make decisions based on what God directs.

You might be wondering, *Just how do I navigate all the opinions and make decisions based on what's best for my family?* Here's a fundamental truth every mom should realize: Your child is unique, one of a kind, and designed for a specific purpose. He was placed on planet Earth at this time in history for a divine appointment. Let that sink in a moment. Based on that truth and the fact that you are his mom, I want you to feel a surge of responsibility.

You, Mom, should make it your mission to be a student of your children to determine what their gifts and talents are, and *you* should foster those gifts and talents and help them believe in themselves exactly the way God made them.

Given that truth, when faced with a mound of choices, you throw out, initially, anything and everything that isn't in line with how your child is gifted. You completely ignore what everyone else's kid is doing, and you home in on what your child's bent is. This can be as easy as noticing that your child always seems to want to color . . . Do you have a right-brained future artist on your hands? Invest in a few arts-and-crafts supplies and see if she thrives and keeps coming back for more.

That may mean that when everyone else is signing up for a third season of soccer, and you've noticed she doesn't "love" soccer like everyone else, you give her a choice: soccer or art classes at the community center? If she picks art classes, there's your answer. You don't have to sign up for both because everyone else's kid is playing soccer. Signing up for both would mean skipping family meals two nights a week because Dad would have to pick her up from soccer practice after work and then grab fast food on the way home.

Instead, choose family time *and* go with your daughter's natural bent. Art classes on Wednesdays! Family meals at home every other night of the week! Score!

It's so important to help your children have major wins in areas where they are naturally gifted. Doing things they're good at builds their confidence. Once they're confident in themselves, they'll be more willing to try (and ultimately even thrive at) what they're not so good at.

Here's what I mean: If your son has no rhythm whatsoever, don't sign him up for band just because you were in the band. Allow him to participate with peers in something he's good at so he gets a "major win" around his friends—that boosts his belief in himself. If he's a master thinker and can "kill" at chess, put him on a chess team and watch his confidence rise with every match. Then at home, in the presence of those who love and support him, start introducing him to musical things and help him improve. Who knows? He might end up wanting to play in the band because he has more confidence in that area.

Do you see how instead of the activity driving your child, your child drives the activity? This doesn't mean that you don't challenge your child. What it means is that you give him a major win in the areas where he excels in order to give him confidence to work harder in the areas that don't necessarily come easily to him. Trust me, once filled with confidence, your child will be so comfortable in his own skin that in the areas where he's not gifted, he won't care, because he'll understand that he can't be great at everything, but he can try anything. That's what confidence does for a child.

Thankfully, I'm beginning to see an inclination in moms today to listen to and analyze the voices around them but not blindly follow what others say is best for them or their families. More and more women go through the decision-making process with their husbands (or wise counsel, if they're unmarried) to weigh all factors to determine what is vital for their families. When we look at our options, give serious thought to what is best, and then move forward, we can have confidence in our decisions and, at the same time, model good decision-making to our children.

Teaching Our Children to Make Wise Choices

Have you ever seen a horse with blinders around his eyes? The horse trainer has recognized that his finely trained animal has an amazing propensity to "lose its head," forget everything it was ever taught, and become distracted and led off course. A horse can be so led astray that it will fail to do what it has been designed and trained to do. Just as horses can head in the wrong direction because they're going with the flow, fearful of the crowd, or in flat out defiance from too much stimulation, so, too, can our children.

A horse's blinders allow the animal to focus on the guidance being offered by the one it can trust. Moms, we have to teach our children to live their lives with blinders on—world blinders. The question isn't whether our kids will be tempted or led astray—we can expect that to happen. The question is, When they are led off course, what decisions will they make?

Horses generally have no need for blinders in their everyday lives, but on race day or when they're in the big city pulling a carriage, blinders are applied to give a horse the security of focusing on the person it should place its reliance and trust in. Talk to your children about the very real truth that there is a path God has intended for them, but there will also be distractions and temptations designed to veer them away from that course. Train them to listen to and learn from trainers—you, godly friends, trusted adults—and when they're out on the "track" with all the other horses, or in the "big city" with all the distractions, they'll be able to put on their world blinders and focus on where God is leading them.

My daughter always dreamed of being a counselor at Pine Cove Christian Camps and applied for a special counselor program that is offered only after a candidate's senior year of high school. However, as summer approached, she started to feel that she wanted to just have fun during the summer and maybe didn't really want to accept the coveted position she was offered.

We asked her to think about why she suddenly didn't want something she had wanted for so many years. We asked her to discuss it with other godly friends and mentors to explore the reason for her sudden change of heart. She also had a very good conversation with us and was willing to hear our input. She ultimately realized that she had veered off her path. She accepted the position, and that summer at Pine Cove led to an amazing spiritual awakening in her life—no wonder the voices of the world were trying to pull her off course.

As your children are growing up, if you foster open discussion about all aspects of their lives, and if you train them to accept

mom truth ○○○○○○○○○○○○○○○○○○○○○

The world around me is crowded with views, voices, and vices, and each is trying to influence me and my role as a mom. You need to focus on God's mandate for you as a woman and a mother, search your own heart, and seek godly guidance to determine what God's best is for your life and your children's lives.

wisdom from you and other positive influences, you will equip them with powerful world blinders that will keep them on course. Make a habit of talking with your children, not *at* your children. They need training, not dictating; shepherding, not cowboying.

Getting Back on Track

What do I do when I've made the wrong choice? How do I help my children when they make wrong choices? First, don't be discouraged, Mom. We all make wrong decisions at times or regret choices we've made. What matters is how we move forward when that happens.

I remember, years ago, a woman who was about fifteen years older than I whom I used to hope and pray I would become like. She seemed so wise and able to easily make right decisions. It was as though she lived in the center of God's will. I ended up learning that the reason she was so good at making decisions was because of her ability to acknowledge when she had made a wrong one and then adjust her course. That afforded her amazing wisdom.

Honestly, flat out, straight up, if you want to have wisdom beyond your years, you must practice humility. The key to humility is being able to admit when you're wrong, face bad choices and bad decisions, learn from them, and rechart your course based on what God expects of you.

I would be a wealthy woman if I had a nickel for every time I said to my children (and myself), "Okay, you messed up; you made a bad choice. God wants us to learn from our mistakes. So what did you learn from that bad choice?" We have done this since . . . well, since forever. One of our son's regular prayers from the time he was a little boy has been, "God, please help me to make good choices."

Actually, just recently my husband and I had to have a talk with our son over a bad grade. Our son was able to articulate very clearly the choice he had made not to study and why he made it. Then, a few nights later, he was sitting and studying for the weekly quiz he had chosen to ignore the week before. That's a sign of growing in wisdom.

If we had just let it go and not made our son uncomfortable by discussing his bad choice and why he made it, I'm guessing the studying a few nights later wouldn't have happened because he wouldn't have learned from his mistake. He would have just repeated it. And then gotten grounded for a bad grade. Wisdom beats punishment any day!

Mistakes don't occur so that we can cover them over or shame our children; they occur so that we can help our children grow in wisdom. It's a foolish individual who avoids wisdom. It's a courageous individual who owns up to mistakes and faces them head-on in order to grow in character and wisdom.

At times you have to remind your children of their own history. On a very basic level, your child has been set on a course largely due to the fact that she is a part of your family. If you've taken the time and care to pour wisdom, love, and affection into your child's life, then her history will play a positive role in determining her future. Helping your child to see and appreciate that her past leads to her future can steer your child back on track when she's feeling a little lost. That's true for all of us.

As adults, we can be overwhelmed by the voices and messages inundating us. When that happens, we need to pause and remember who we are, what we stand for, and what's important to us. When *you* need to get back on track, Mom, take some time to reflect on what God has already taught you through your life experiences. Maybe you need to find a time to talk with your husband about how you're feeling and decide together what course will work best for your family. You might need to schedule a coffee date with a mentor or a close friend to gain some fresh perspective.

The next time you hear someone tell you, "Well, you know, *they say* . . ." remember that what everyone else says doesn't really matter. Listening to what God says will keep your life on track.

be the mom

They-Say-Mom-Trap Quiz

Please read the following statements and rate yourself on a scale from one (strongly agree) to five (strongly disagree). Then answer the corresponding questions or follow the instructions.

1. I am able to make decisions for myself and my family (with my husband's help, if I'm married) without listening to what "they say." _____

   Write down each of your immediate family members' names; then ask each person, If you could spend each day doing three things, what would those things be?

2. I take time to enjoy the special MOMents of the day, resting in and soaking in the love of my children. _____

   Recall special MOMents of love and write them down.

3. The world's message of putting self first is apparent to me, but I try hard to make decisions based on God's best, not based on what I want. _____

List areas where you have conformed to what the world heralds as best, and determine what you can do to stand against the tendency to conform.

4. My family does not follow the pattern of the world. _____

In what areas of your life do you need "world blinders" so that you and your children may more easily follow God's pattern rather than the world's?

5. I am able to admit the bad choices I make and learn from them. _____

Confess a few of your bad choices. Consider what God
may have been teaching you through those choices.
Grow from those experiences; don't beat yourself up
over them.

Scoring Chart

5–8 = You fully understand that the world tries to influence
you and your decision making, but you are able to
hear God's voice above the world's.

9–12 = You recognize the world's influence and are working
to be set apart (along with your family).

13–16 = You are aware that the influence of the world is sway-
ing you, but you are allowing your best possible life
to be altered by the world's standards.

17–20 = You are dangerously close to being trapped; you
need to change course.

21–25 = You are bound in the They Say Mom trap, and you
need to break free.

Next Up . . .

Just how do we get past the mom traps and be the mom? For me, it took years of trial and error to move forward with joy and hope despite my failures. One traumatic experience gave me the stead-fastness to do so. Read on as I share that story with you.

CHAPTER 9

Be the Mom

My plan for the weekend was moving along just as I had wanted it to. Our home was decorated for Christmas; I had spent the day baking the "family favorite" chocolate chip pumpkin muffins; and both children had napped and were now filled with excitement because their evening was going to be spent with friends who had agreed to babysit.

My favorite little black dress was laid out on the bed in our master bedroom. The blue velvet box that held my prized pearl necklace had been moved from its hiding place and set on the dresser. A tinge of excitement surged through me as I thought of gliding my feet into the so-cute black heels that longed to be danced in. I eagerly anticipated wriggling into my dress, donning the classic pearls, and slipping on the sleek heels—a Cinderella-like transformation. I knew that once I had gone through this simple routine, I would feel more like a woman and less like a mom, until the clock struck midnight. In a mere three hours, I could enjoy that transformation and the anticipated evening with my prince charming at his company Christmas party.

For now, back to momlife for a few more hours.

I was headed down the stairs with my twenty-two-month-old son. As was his custom, he lay on his belly and started his adorable swift-belly scoot down the stairs. I was maybe three steps down the stairway when it happened. His little body abruptly stopped halfway down the stairs as his flailing feet caught on a stair. I watched in stunned horror as momentum sent him through the air, headfirst toward the foot of the stairway. I thrust my arms forward as if my will to catch him from the top of the stairs would somehow soften his fall as he hit the hard wooden floor at the bottom of the stairs.

The sound of his head hitting the floor thundered in my eardrums like a sledgehammer. I yelled my husband's name and was instantly by my son on the floor, gently whispering in his ear.

Nothing.

My husband quickly appeared at my side. He picked up our son. He was unresponsive. Then our son threw up. His eyes were open, but they were glassy, vacant.

We immediately left for the doctor's office. Our friends met us there and took our daughter home with them. The doctor saw my son as soon as we got there and then sent us straight to the hospital, insisting that we could get there faster than an ambulance. He would meet us there.

The next several hours were a bit of a blur. Many tests. Doctors. Nurses. Voices. My only clear memory was of my son's eyes—distant, unfocused, unrecognizing. Where was my boy?

I begged God, *If You'll spare him, I'll do whatever it takes. I'll change the diapers of a five-year-old, a twelve-year-old, a twenty-two-year-old. I can do this. Just don't let him die.*

I was resigned to the fact that I would do anything for this little boy who had brought joy and adventure to our home from the moment he was born.

I will do anything, sacrifice anything, day after day, for my son. I am his mom. Please, please, please.

I heard a guitar and singing coming down the hall. Three clowns walked to our doorway, a nurse whispered something to them, and they were silent. I later learned that they were praying for my son.

They began to play and sing softly. Then the most beautiful thing happened, my son's eyes changed. My boy looked right at me, and he saw me. He came back to me. His little arms reached up for me, he looked at the clowns, he looked at me, and then he began to cry, clinging to me. I wept at the sweet sound of his crying. My husband cried and cradled us both.

The clowns referred to my son as their Christmas-miracle baby. And to this day, I understand more clearly the gift of motherhood, and I'm grateful to *be the mom*.

You Can Do This

This memory reminds me of what my mothering can look like when I'm concentrating on loving my child and being grateful to God for my child. The frustrations and aggravations I face daily are somehow more easily received when I have "what could have been" etched into my mind. Even more so when I read about mothers or meet mothers who have so much more to bear than most. A mom, when faced with children who present unique challenges, will so often exhibit courage and seemingly impossible strength for the sake of her child. We could all learn the true meaning of selflessness by spending time with such moms.

We each have our own story; no story is more important than another. God is the One who sees and knows; He is the One who waits for you to seek Him in the midst of your story. No matter the challenges you face, or will face, as a mom, you have been divinely equipped to face them and grow through them. God is the Potter and you are the clay. He is molding and fashioning you and, through you, your children. That truth holds great beauty and divine security.

Some people out there refer to themselves as mom experts—well, I am no expert but I am a mom witness. A witness to what God can do for you and through you if you allow Him to.

This Is Personal

My general nature and attitude in life are high energy, fun-loving, and joy-filled. But I have inner struggles and battles I fight that spill out all over my family—pride, selfishness, and so on. I need God to daily help me be more like Jesus.

I started writing this book for my daughter because I feared that when she becomes a mom and begins falling into the mom traps, she'll think she isn't "cut out" to be a mom. I don't want you to think that either. When you're in the thick of it and think, *This is just too hard; I can't do this,* you need to know I thought that too. When you're tempted to follow the world's choices, I want you to hear God's voice above all the noise.

I've exposed my own shortcomings and put these hard mom lessons on paper to help you understand the truth about being a mom. You, too, will become entrenched in the traps unless you draw close to God. You will be overwhelmed by the voices all around you unless you determine to stay focused on God's will for you and your family. You need to know that as you seek to obey Him, God will mold you and grow you into the powerful woman He wants you to be. I've met countless moms who have struggled with the mom traps, and as they will testify, knowledge leads to freedom.

Being the Mom

There are no perfect moms, and there are no tips or suggestions that will make you the world's best mom. But there are practical steps and training that can embolden you to stay the course.

A few years ago I got it in my head that I would train for a half marathon. It was so hard. I had to work to build up my cardiovascular endurance and my muscle strength. In the midst of training, I consistently told myself that it was too hard and I should quit, not even try. There were plenty of other things I could be doing during my 5:00 AM training runs. But I'm hardheaded and just stubborn enough to force myself to keep at it. You know what happened? I did grow in endurance and strength because I kept up the training and the suffering even when it was hard. I knew that what I was doing was strengthening me to finish the race well.

I get that momlife isn't always easy. But I want you to understand, Mom, that even the hard times are worth it. Romans 5:3-4 says, "We also rejoice in our sufferings, because we know that suffering produces perseverance; perseverance, character; and character, hope." I'll take perseverance, character, and hope over a medal for a half marathon any day! (But the medal is shiny, and I did get one!)

mom truth ○○○○○○○○○○○○○○○○○○○○

I've learned that I am building a legacy as I raise my children. C. S. Lewis said, "The homemaker has the ultimate career. All other careers exist for one purpose only, and that is to support the ultimate career."[1] Mom, these quippy "mom trap" names do not define you and who you are, but giving them names helps you see them for what they are—traps waiting to ensnare you. We all fall into these traps, but God is able to set us free!

There are four very practical faith steps you can take to hear from God as He equips you to be the mom.

1. Spend time each day in prayer. If prayer isn't currently part of your life, you may begin by reading the Psalms aloud and then thanking God for your many blessings and praying for your children.

2. Find yourself a mentor, a mom who is older than you and further along in her faith journey, and ask her to meet with you weekly or monthly. This mentoring relationship can work in person, by phone, or even through the Internet with a friend or a trained mentor. If you would like a mom e-mentor, go to *www.momlifetoday. com/ementoring/* for more information.

3. Seek out opportunities to serve in ways that further God's kingdom. Through that process, God will begin to reveal His desire for your momlife and His plan for your future.

4. Study God's Word daily, recognizing the many ways this can happen, such as sitting down with your Bible and reading by yourself, participating in a regular Bible study, writing Scripture passages on note cards and placing them around your home, reading your children's Bible with them, or listening to hymns and praise music. There are even online Bible studies available by several well-known authors. Try sites like *www. womensbiblecafe.com*. The point is, make time every day to meditate on God's Word, but don't get caught up in thinking there's only one way to do this. It can lead to discouragement if you can't do it your preferred way. Use a variety of methods to get the Word of God into your heart, which will indeed allow Him to work in your life.

The Creator of the heavens and the earth fashioned you to be the mother of the children He has entrusted to you. What joy it is to embrace the role of motherhood, free ourselves from the traps that aim to devour and devalue us, and live a momlife worthy of His calling. This doesn't mean a momlife without challenges or mistakes, but a momlife increasingly dependent upon our heavenly Father. Not expecting perfection but being willing to love and nurture our children, to help them grow into the women and men God intends for them to be.

A mom gives life through the birth of her child and molds that life through the love and attention she provides her child. What a privilege it is to hear, "I love you, Mom!" spoken from little cherub lips that never tire of repeating that phrase over and over. What a joy "Love ya!" is when it is heard in the deep, gravelly voice of a teenage boy.

The truth you must cling to is this: Whether or not you are currently feeling valued as a mom doesn't detract from the fact that you *are*! Your Father in heaven sees you, appreciates you, and celebrates you for who you are! Mom, hear these four very real faith truths, and hear them loud and clear:

1. You matter. You are loved. There is a God who loves you. Loves, loves, loves you! Let that sink in.
2. You are not alone. God has placed other moms in your life who understand. They'll help you if you ask for help.
3. You are God's hands. God knows each day with children is hard, challenging, wonderful, and overwhelming—all at the same time. You are to be the gentle hand that daily guides and teaches. He expects you to take the good with the bad and realize that if you lean on Him and learn not to require too much of yourself (or your children), you can find joy and grow through the hard moments.

4. You have much value. God made you unique, just the way you are, and He knew you were the perfect mom for your children. God is right by your side every day, shouting His love for you through your child's giggle, through butterfly kisses, and through the aches of your mom heart.

God notices you, loves you, and delights over you. Daily. He sees you. When you're experiencing suffering, hurt, and unhappiness, feeling that no one understands who you are or your value, recognize that God is there. He can empower, strengthen, and hold you up.

If you've never taken the time to reflect on the truth that motherhood is a gift to grow your children and you, it is my heart's desire that right now you'll allow yourself that luxury. Think about what it means to *be the mom*. The gift God has given you and what He reveals of Himself through motherhood should fill you with wonder and anticipation. Each day you spend raising your precious children is an opportunity to lean into God's love for you and share His love with your children. It really is the best job in the world.

Questions for Reflection
or Discussion

1. Share your mom story, your journey to motherhood.

2. Think about the obvious ways God has chosen you to be the mom to the children He has entrusted to you. Write down a few here.

3. Do you recognize that God uses motherhood and the frustrations that accompany it to mold you into the woman He wants you to be? List areas where you have experienced growth as a direct result of your frustrations as a mom.

4. Will you commit to the four faith steps that will train you to be the mother God wants you to be? These are the new PMS's in your life—Praying, Mentoring, Serving, Studying—that will get you through the day with a joyful attitude! Is there anything else you want to commit to as you move forward? If so, write that down now.

5. Will you believe the four faith truths that are true about you?
   - You matter. I, _____ (fill in your name), matter to God.
   - You are not alone. I have other women in my life who are willing to come alongside me. I will pray about and contact _____ and share that I need advice and a caring friend.
   - You are God's hands. God sees me, _____ (fill in your name), and He is with me always, growing me through my role as mom.
   - You have much value. God purposefully gave me, _____ (fill in your name), my children,
   _____
   _____ (fill in children's names), because He knew that I was uniquely and divinely designed to be the mom to my children.

Notes

Preface

1. Helen Reddy and Ray Burton, "I Am Woman," copyright © 1971.

Chapter 2

1. C. S. Lewis, *The Screwtape Letters* (New York: Harper Collins, 2001), 155.
2. Paul Bedard, "Report: College Dropouts Rob Feds of Millions," *U.S. News & World Report*, August 22, 2011, http://www .usnews.com/news/blogs/washington-whispers/2011/08/22 /report-college-dropouts-rob-feds-of-billions.

Chapter 4

1. Jennifer's blog post. Used by permission.
2. Richard M. Sherman and Robert B. Sherman, "The Wonderful Thing About Tiggers," copyright © 1968.
3. Francesca Battistelli, "Free to Be Me," *My Paper Heart*, copyright © 2009, Word Entertainment LLC.

Chapter 5

1. Jon Acuff, *Quitter* (Brenton: Lampo Press/The Lampo Group, Inc., 2011), 93-94.

Chapter 6

1. The Barna Group, "Survey Reveals the Life Christians Desire," July 21, 2008, http://www.barna.org/congregations-articles /29-survey-reveals-the-life-christians-desire (http://www.barna .org). Used by permission.

2. Kathryn Stockett, *The Help* (New York: Penguin Group, 2011).

3. Dennis Rainey and Barbara Rainey, *Moments with You: Daily Connections for Couples* (Ventura, CA: Regal Books, 2011).

Chapter 7

1. Tim Elmore, *Generation iY: Our Last Chance to Save Their Future* (Atlanta: Poet Gardener Publishing, 2010), 45.

2. Personal story shared by Barbara Rainey. Used by permission.

3. Personal story shared by Karen Loritts. Used by permission.

Chapter 9

1. C. S. Lewis (1898-1963), http://www.goodreads.com /quotes/show/20606.

About the Author

Tracey Eyster is the creator and editor of MomLife Today (*www.mom lifetoday.com*). Tenacity and a passion for momlife have fueled her relentless pursuit of following God's call to speak wisdom and truth into the lives of moms through writing and speaking. She delights in doing video interviews and exploring momlife with all types of moms. Tracey enjoys exploring the outdoors through hiking, horseback riding, and kayaking. She is a chai tea sipper, half-marathon completer, banana grams dominator, dust bunny gatherer, and home cookin' preparer who seeks authentic relationships—life's too important for fluff! She's been a mom for more than eighteen years, and she and her husband, Bill, have been married for twenty-five years. You can visit Tracey at *www.traceyster.com* or connect with her on Facebook at Be the Mom.

All author proceeds for Tracey's *Be the Mom* book will go to Project 319 at Pine Cove Christian Camps (Tyler, Texas).

○   ○   ○

Thank you for purchasing this book – you just helped send a child or family in need to camp! Tracey's proceeds are being given to Project 319, Pine Cove's scholarship program.

"IF YOU SPEND YOURSELVES ON BEHALF OF THE HUNGRY AND SATISFY THE NEEDS OF THE OPPRESSED THEN YOUR LIGHT WILL RISE IN THE DARKNESS AND YOUR NIGHT WILL BE LIKE THE NOON DAY."
– ISAIAH 58:10

Project 319 provides scholarships to youth who are considered at-risk, active military families and campers in spiritual and financial need.

Never wanting to turn a child or family in need away, Project 319 is being used by God to bring about Christ-centered change to hurting children and families who need the refreshing touch of Jesus. They will see and hear the Gospel message through education, worship, counseling, relationships, and recreation in the beautiful woods of East and South Texas.

Project 319 offers opportunity for a life transformed. Many will never be the same.

"Pine Cove exists to be used by God to transform the lives of people for His purposes and His glory."

FOCUS ON THE FAMILY®

Welcome to the Family

Whether you purchased this book, borrowed it, or received it as a gift, thanks for reading it! This is just one of many insightful, biblically based resources that Focus on the Family produces for people in all stages of life.

Focus is a global Christian ministry dedicated to helping families thrive as they celebrate and cultivate God's design for marriage and experience the adventure of parenthood. Our outreach exists to support individuals and families in the joys and challenges they face, and to equip and empower them to be the best they can be.

Through our many media outlets, we offer help and hope, promote moral values and share the life-changing message of Jesus Christ with people around the world.

Focus on the Family MAGAZINES

These faith-building, character-developing publications address the interests, issues, concerns, and challenges faced by every member of your family from preschool through the senior years.

For More INFORMATION

ONLINE:
Log on to
FocusOnTheFamily.com
In Canada, log on to
FocusOnTheFamily.ca

PHONE:
Call toll-free:
**800-A-FAMILY
(232-6459)**
In Canada, call toll-free:
800-661-9800

THRIVING FAMILY®	FOCUS ON	FOCUS ON	FOCUS ON
Marriage & Parenting	THE FAMILY CLUBHOUSE JR.® Ages 4 to 8	THE FAMILY CLUBHOUSE® Ages 8 to 12	THE FAMILY CITIZEN® U.S. news issues

Rev. 3/11

More expert resources
for marriage and parenting . . .

Do you want to be a better parent? Enjoy a stronger marriage? Focus on the Family's collection of inspiring, practical, resources can help your family grow closer and stronger than ever before. Whichever format you might need—video, audio, book or e-book, we have something for you. Visit our online Family Store and discover how we can help your family thrive at **FocusOnTheFamily.com/resources**.